THE ICE CIDER EPIC
A HISTORY & COOKBOOK

ISBN
978-1-989647-40-0

© 2023 R.H. Mason
A Byrd Press Publication
Toronto
www.byrdpress.com
publisher@byrdpress.com

Art Direction Avery Martin

THE ICE CIDER EPIC
A HISTORY & COOKBOOK

Introduction to Ice Cider

Ice cider, also known as "cidre de glace," is a unique and flavorful beverage that originated in Quebec in the early 1990s. It is the cider equivalent of ice wine, made from the sweet juice of frozen apples, similar to the process of making ice wine from frozen grapes. The idea of ice cider was first conceived by Christian Barthomeuf, a winemaker from Quebec, who was inspired by the production of ice wines in Germany. The harsh Quebec winters and the abundance of apple orchards in the region made it an ideal place for the creation of this distinctive beverage.

The first official bottle of ice cider, produced by La Ciderie St.-Nicholas, appeared in a Quebec government-run liquor store in 1999, marking the recognition of this new beverage. The production of ice cider has since expanded, with over 60 producers in Quebec alone, and has inspired producers in other regions with similar climatic conditions. Today, ice cider is also produced in Western Canada, Europe, and the United States, reflecting its growing popularity and influence.

The process of making ice cider involves the fermentation of the concentrated juice of frozen apples, resulting in a beverage with a higher alcohol content than traditional cider. The unique climate and natural resources of Quebec, as well as other regions with freezing temperatures, contribute to the exceptional quality of ice cider. The beverage has gained recognition in high-end restaurants and has become a sought-after product for its rich, fruity, and velvety taste.

The history and development of ice cider showcase its cultural and geographical significance, making it a distinctive and cherished product of the regions where it is produced. The combination of natural factors, innovative techniques, and the vision of its creators has led to the establishment of ice cider as a premium and sought-after beverage, enjoyed by connoisseurs and enthusiasts around the world.

Acknowledgment to Domaine Leduc-Piedimonte

Domaine Leduc-Piedimonte, nestled in the picturesque Rougemont, Quebec, stands as a renowned artisanal producer of ice cider. Co-founded in 2004 by Robert McKeown and Andrée St-Denis, this cidery has earned acclaim for crafting ciders that are both rich and complex. Utilizing a method unique to Quebec, Leduc-Piedimonte's ice cider is created by harnessing the natural concentration of overripe apples induced by the region's cold temperatures. The result is a highly sought-after beverage celebrated for its exceptional taste profile.

The ice cider from Leduc-Piedimonte tantalizes the palate with a rich and intricate flavor experience. Its unctuousness is delicately balanced by the nuances of caramelized citrus fruit and apricot, culminating in a gentle acidity complemented by subtle maple notes. This golden amber elixir releases delightful aromas of orange zest, butter, honey, and spicy vanilla. Described as fruity and extra sweet, the cider reflects the distinct concentration of flavors derived from apples ripened to perfection by the cold. Overall, Leduc-Piedimonte's ice cider presents a full-bodied, fruity sweetness with a harmonious balance of acidity and aromatic notes, making it a truly distinctive and cherished beverage.

The cidery's commitment to quality, coupled with the bounty of Quebec's apples and freezing winter temperatures, has solidified Leduc-Piedimonte's ice cider as a sought-after choice among enthusiasts and connoisseurs worldwide.

I am deeply grateful to Leduc-Piedimonte for their steadfast support and inspiration during the research, development, and test kitchen phases of this project. Their exceptional ice cider, with its unique characteristics and rich, complex taste profile, has played a pivotal role in guiding the original and uncharted culinary journey presented in this book.

Leduc-Piedimonte's dedication to harnessing Quebec's abundant apples and frigid winter temperatures not only influenced the content of this book but also served as a driving force in exploring the incorporation of ice cider into a variety of historic and contemporary recipes. This endeavor mirrors the culinarily adventurous spirit embodied by Leduc-Piedimonte and reflects the philosophy inherent in their remarkable ice cider.

The distinctive features of Leduc-Piedimonte's ice cider, including its unctuousness, caramelized citrus fruit and apricot flavors, light and pleasant acidity, and the natural concentration of flavors from overripe apples transformed by the cold, have significantly enriched the content of this book. They offer readers a deeper understanding and appreciation of this exceptional beverage.

Once again, I extend my heartfelt gratitude to Leduc-Piedimonte for their instrumental role in encouraging this innovative exploration and for being an integral part of the creative process. Their commitment to producing outstanding ice cider has not only elevated the culinary landscape but has also served as an inspiration for the captivating journey presented in this book.

An Invitation

Welcome to "The Ice Cider Epic: A History & Cookbook" where we revel in the extraordinary infusion of ice cider into our culinary world. This book is an invitation to explore the kitchen's heart, where ice cider becomes a transformative ingredient in both historic and contemporary recipes.

Here's why we're thrilled to share this culinary adventure:

1. Culinary Exploration: This collection invites you on a journey, featuring a diverse range of recipes that showcase the incredible ways ice cider can enhance both sweet and savory dishes.

2. Showcasing Ice Cider's Depth: More than a beverage, ice cider is a symphony of tastes—blending sweetness, acidity, and fruity notes. Through these recipes, we aim to spotlight the depth and complexity that ice cider brings to the culinary table.

3. Pairing Possibilities: Discover the art of pairing as we guide you through combinations that elevate both the dish and the ice cider. Uncover the secrets of creating harmonious flavor profiles to enhance your culinary repertoire.

4. Dessert and Beverage Enhancements: Explore the versatility of ice cider in desserts and beverages, where it becomes a key player. From drizzling it over pastries to crafting refreshing beverages, these recipes showcase its diverse applications.

5. Seasonal Inspirations: Embrace the changing seasons with recipes that capture each time of year's essence. From cozy winter evenings to vibrant summer gatherings, ice cider seamlessly integrates into dishes reflecting the spirit of the season.

6. Sharing the Joy of Cooking with Ice Cider: Cooking is a shared experience that brings people together. This book encourages you to share the joy of cooking and savoring ice cider-infused creations with loved ones, fostering a sense of community and celebration.

7. Culinary Artistry: Ice cider isn't just an ingredient; it's a form of culinary art. These recipes inspire your own culinary artistry, providing a canvas for you to express creativity and transform everyday ingredients into extraordinary dishes.

Whether you're a seasoned chef or a home cook eager to experiment, "The Ice Cider Epic" invites you to unlock the full potential of ice cider in the kitchen. Let these pages be your guide to a journey that promises to delight your taste buds, inspire your creativity, and elevate your appreciation for this golden nectar. Cheers to the art of culinary crafting with ice cider!

for Quebec

Table of Contents

Overview of Ice Cider...1

100 Foods That Pair Well with Ice Cider...7

Contemporary Ice Cider Recipes inspired by the Ancient Romans...8

Contemporary Ice Cider Recipes inspired by the Medieval Culinary Traditions...19

Contemporary Ice Cider Recipes inspired by the Renaissance Culinary Traditions...30

Contemporary Ice Cider Recipes inspired by the Savory Victorian Culinary Traditions...41

Contemporary Ice Cider Recipes inspired by the Sweet Victorian Culinary Traditions...53

Contemporary Ice Cider Recipes inspired by North American Cuisine...63

Contemporary Ice Cider Recipes inspired by Pacific Rim Cuisine... 75

Contemporary Ice Cider Recipes inspired by Chinese Cuisine...86

Two Cocktails...100

Bonus Recipes ...102

Final Thoughts ...126

Overview of Ice Cider

The Essence of Ice Cider

Nature's Bounty and Human Ingenuity:

Ice cider, a delightful and luxurious beverage, embodies the harmonious relationship between nature's bounty and human ingenuity. The foundation of ice cider lies in the inherent sweetness and complexity of apples, nature's gift to orchard dwellers. Orchards, with their rows of flourishing apple trees, bear witness to the seasonal dance between sunlight, rain, and the earth's nurturing embrace.

As the apples ripen on the branches, they accumulate natural sugars and flavors that form the backbone of ice cider. The unique terroir of the orchard, influenced by soil composition, climate, and apple varieties, imparts distinct characteristics to the final elixir. Nature provides the raw materials, but it is human cultivation and stewardship that transform these humble apples into a symphony of flavors.

Human ingenuity comes into play during the meticulous process of harvesting and pressing the apples. Apples chosen for ice cider production are often left to linger on the trees well into the winter months. The frost-kissed apples, concentrated by the cold, yield a nectar rich in sugars and aromas. The careful selection of apples and the timing of their harvest are crucial steps in coaxing out the finest qualities from nature's bounty.

Tradition and Innovation: A Harmonious Marriage:

Ice cider production is a testament to the seamless blend of tradition and innovation. Drawing inspiration from age-old techniques, cidermakers have revived and refined the art of making ice cider, paying homage to the traditions of their predecessors. These methods, rooted in the wisdom of generations, form the backbone of the craft, ensuring a connection to the past that enriches the present.

In tandem with tradition, innovative techniques and modern equipment elevate the craft of ice cider making. Temperature-controlled environments, specialized fermentation vessels, and scientific understanding of yeast strains contribute to the precision and consistency of the final product. This fusion of old-world charm and cutting-edge technology results in a beverage that respects its heritage while embracing the possibilities of the future.

The essence of ice cider lies not only in the sweet elixir it produces but also in the delicate dance between nature's rhythms and human hands. It is a celebration of the orchard's bounty, a toast to the seasons, and a testament to the ingenuity that transforms apples into liquid gold. In each sip, one can taste the culmination of tradition and innovation—a harmonious marriage that encapsulates the spirit of ice cider.

§

The Making of Liquid Gold

Natural Freezing and Concentration of Apple Juice:

The journey to create the liquid gold known as ice cider begins with the natural freezing and concentration of apple juice. In the heart of winter, orchardists patiently await the perfect moment when temperatures plummet, allowing the apples to freeze on the branches. This natural freeze concentrates the sugars and flavors within the apples, creating a nectar that is the essence of sweetness and complexity.

Once the apples are sufficiently frost-kissed, they are carefully handpicked, each one a jewel glistening with the magic of winter. The frozen apples, now bursting with concentrated sugars, are pressed to extract the rich, viscous juice that forms the base of ice cider. This natural concentration process ensures that the liquid gold carries the pure and intensified flavors of the orchard's bounty.

Winter's Embrace: The Meticulous Process:

Winter's embrace extends beyond the orchard to the ciderhouse, where the meticulous process of transforming concentrated apple juice into ice cider unfolds. The cidermaker, armed with the bounty of the winter harvest, oversees every detail with precision and care.

The concentrated apple juice is left to ferment in cold temperatures, allowing the sugars to slowly transform into alcohol. This extended fermentation process, often taking months, imparts depth and complexity to the final product. Patience becomes a virtue as the cidermaker monitors and guides the transformation, ensuring that the alchemy of winter's embrace works its magic on the liquid gold.

As the cider matures, the distinct flavors of the apple varieties and the unique terroir of the orchard become more pronounced. The marriage of winter's chill and the artistry of the cidermaker results in a symphony of tastes that dance on the palate, creating an experience that is both timeless and ephemeral.

Fermentation: Unveiling the Alchemy of Yeast in Ice Cider Production

At the core of crafting ice cider lies the captivating alchemy of yeast. This transformative dance between yeast and sugars is a pivotal step that bequeaths character and effervescence to the liquid gold. Specially curated yeast strains, chosen for their adeptness in thriving within cold temperatures, engage in an enchanting process, deftly converting sugars into alcohol and carbon dioxide.

In this alchemical symphony, the cidermaker assumes the role of conductor, skillfully balancing the interplay of sweetness and acidity to orchestrate the desired harmony. The outcome is a libation that not only captivates the senses but achieves a delicate equilibrium between the innate sweetness of the concentrated juice and the nuanced notes derived from fermentation.

Ultimately, the creation of liquid gold serves as a testament to the intricate interplay of nature, craftsmanship, and the alchemy of fermentation. From the frost-kissed apples adorning the branches to the meticulously nurtured fermentation process, each phase contributes to the formation of a beverage that encapsulates the very essence of winter's magic – a golden elixir that beckons with the promise of indulgence and the comforting warmth of tradition.

§

The Dance of Flavors

Sweetness and Acidity: A Delicate Interplay:

In the captivating world of ice cider, the dance of flavors is a nuanced and intricate performance, where sweetness and acidity engage in a delicate interplay. The concentrated apple juice, born from the frost-kissed apples of winter, lays the foundation for this harmonious duet. The inherent sweetness, a gift from nature's alchemy, is balanced by a subtle acidity that adds brightness and vitality to each sip.

Cidermakers, akin to skilled choreographers, carefully calibrate this interplay during the fermentation process. The slow transformation of sugars into alcohol is guided with finesse, ensuring that sweetness is tempered by a lively acidity. The result is a symphony on the taste buds, where the contrasting elements create a balanced and memorable composition. In the dance of flavors, sweetness and acidity waltz together, leaving a lingering and enchanting impression.

Orchestrating Fruity Notes: A Symphony in Every Sip:

As the liquid gold matures, the orchestration of fruity notes takes center stage, transforming each sip into a symphony of flavors. The concentrated essence of apple varieties, nurtured in the orchard's embrace, unfolds in layers of complexity. The cidermaker, akin to a maestro conducting an orchestra, guides the emergence of distinct fruity notes that contribute to the beverage's richness.

From the crisp, fresh notes of orchard apples to the nuanced undertones of pear or quince, each flavor contributes to the composition. The dance of flavors extends beyond the orchard, incorporating hints of honey, caramel, or spice that arise from the fermentation and aging process. The result is a sensory experience that transcends the ordinary, inviting connoisseurs to savor the symphony in every nuanced sip.

Complexity Born from Natural Concentration:

In the world of ice cider, the dance of flavors is a sensory journey, inviting enthusiasts to partake in a symphony of sweetness, acidity, and nuanced fruity notes. Each sip is a step in this elegant dance, a moment of pure indulgence that reflects the mastery of the cidermaker and the richness of the orchard's bounty. The complexity of ice cider is a result of the intricate and natural concentration process that occurs during the frosty embrace of winter. This process is fundamental to the creation of a beverage that transcends the ordinary, offering a symphony of flavors that captivate the palate.

The natural concentration begins in the orchard, where apples are left on the trees to weather the winter chill. As temperatures drop, the water content in the apples freezes, leaving behind a higher concentration of sugars, acids, and other compounds. This natural concentration is a slow, transformative dance that takes place over weeks, if not months, under the whims of winter's grasp.

§

Craftsmanship and Authenticity

Regions of Thriving Orchards:

Craftsmanship and authenticity are deeply intertwined in the world of ice cider, and they find their roots in the regions of thriving orchards. The geographical location of orchards plays a crucial role in shaping the unique character of ice cider. Orchards nestled in specific climates, soils, and altitudes contribute distinct terroirs, infusing the final product with the essence of the land.

Regions known for their thriving orchards, such as Quebec in Canada, Vermont in the United States, or Normandy in France, have become epicenters of ice cider craftsmanship. The cool climates and fertile landscapes of these areas provide an ideal environment for apple cultivation, resulting in fruit with a nuanced flavor profile. Craftsmen in these regions draw inspiration from their orchards, utilizing the natural elements of the land to create ice cider that is a true reflection of its origin.

The Role of Apple Varieties in Crafting:

Craftsmanship in ice cider extends to the careful selection and blending of apple varieties. Each apple brings a unique set of flavors, aromas, and acidity to the blend, contributing to the complexity of the final product. Craftsmen often blend a combination of sweet, tart, and aromatic apple varieties to achieve a well-balanced and nuanced flavor profile.

The choice of apple varieties is a meticulous process that requires an intimate knowledge of each cultivar's characteristics. From heirloom varieties with rich histories to modern hybrids bred for specific qualities, the diverse palette of apples allows craftsmen to create a symphony of flavors. The art lies not just in the selection but in the precise orchestration of these varieties to achieve a harmonious and authentic expression of the orchard's bounty.

Ice Cider as Craft and Authentic Expression:

Ice cider is not merely a beverage; it is a craft and an authentic expression of the cidermaker's skill and connection to the land. Craftsmanship is evident in every step of the process, from the patient waiting for the frost to work its magic on the apples to the meticulous pressing, fermentation, and aging. Each decision, from the choice of apples to the timing of harvest, reflects the craftsman's dedication to quality and authenticity.

The authenticity of ice cider lies in its genuine connection to the orchard and its surroundings. Craftsmen often embrace traditional methods passed down through generations, paying homage to the roots of the craft. This commitment to authenticity goes hand in hand with innovation, as craftsmen find ways to elevate and refine their techniques while preserving the essence of the artisanal process.

In essence, ice cider is a living testament to craftsmanship and authenticity. It is a celebration of the regions that nurture thriving orchards, a symphony composed from carefully selected apple varieties, and a craft that embodies the genuine expression of a cidermaker's passion and connection to the land. Each bottle of ice cider is not just a product; it is a story, a journey, and a true reflection of the artistry that transforms apples into liquid gold.

Approaching Food Pairings with Ice Cider:

Pairing ice cider with food is an art that involves understanding the intricate flavors, textures, and nuances of both the beverage and the dishes. Ice cider's sweet, complex, and often fruity profile makes it a versatile companion to a range of culinary delights. The key to successful food pairings lies in complementing and contrasting the flavors, creating a harmonious experience for the palate.

Why Some Foods Pair Well with Ice Cider:

1. Cheese: Rich and creamy cheeses, such as brie or blue cheese, complement the sweetness of ice cider. The contrast in textures and flavors creates a delightful balance on the palate. The acidity of the cider also helps cut through the richness of the cheese, enhancing the overall tasting experience.

2. Spicy Foods: Ice cider's sweetness serves as a pleasant counterpoint to the heat of spicy dishes. Whether it's spicy Thai cuisine or Mexican dishes, the sweetness can help soothe the palate and provide a refreshing contrast.

3. Foie Gras and Pâté: The luscious and savory nature of foie gras or pâté pairs well with the sweetness and acidity of ice cider. The combination elevates both the food and the beverage, creating a luxurious tasting experience.

4. Desserts: Ice cider is often a dessert in itself, but it can also complement a variety of sweet treats. Pairing it with desserts such as apple pie, caramel-based sweets, or fruit tarts enhances the overall sweetness and brings out the fruity notes in the cider.

5. Pork and Poultry: Ice cider's sweet and fruity characteristics work well with the savory flavors of pork and poultry dishes. Whether it's roasted chicken, glazed ham, or pork tenderloin, the pairing can create a balanced and flavorful ensemble.

Why Some Foods Might Not Pair Well:

1. Overpowering Flavors: Foods with overpowering flavors, such as extremely spicy dishes or those with strong, pungent ingredients, may overshadow the delicate nuances of ice cider. It's essential to balance the intensity of both the food and the beverage.

2. Highly Tannic Dishes: Ice cider often lacks the tannins found in some traditional wines, so pairing it with highly tannic dishes might result in a clash of flavors. Tannins can sometimes accentuate bitterness or astringency, disrupting the harmonious balance.

3. Oily or Greasy Foods: While some richness is complemented by ice cider, excessively oily or greasy foods may overwhelm the palate. The cider's sweetness may struggle to cut through the heavy textures and flavors of such dishes.

4. Overly Salty Dishes: Ice cider's sweetness can accentuate the perception of saltiness, so excessively salty dishes might clash with the natural sweetness of the beverage. It's crucial to maintain a balanced interplay between sweet and savory.

In essence, the success of food pairings with ice cider lies in finding a delicate balance and understanding the interplay of flavors. Experimentation is encouraged, as personal preferences play a significant role in determining ideal pairings. The beauty of ice cider lies not only in its standalone enjoyment but also in its ability to enhance and elevate the culinary experience when paired thoughtfully with a variety of foods.

100 Foods That Pair Well with Ice Cider

Cheese:
1. Aged Cheddar
2. Blue Cheese
3. Camembert
4. Brie
5. Gouda
6. Roquefort
7. Manchego
8. Goat Cheese
9. Gruyère
10. Stilton

Charcuterie:
11. Prosciutto
12. Salami
13. Soppressata
14. Chorizo
15. Duck Pâté
16. Serrano Ham
17. Capicola
18. Mortadella
19. Coppa
20. Speck

Fruits:
21. Apples
22. Pears
23. Berries (Strawberries, Blueberries, Raspberries)
24. Figs
25. Grapes
26. Apricots
27. Persimmons
28. Quince
29. Cherries
30. Pineapple

Nuts:
31. Walnuts
32. Almonds
33. Pecans
34. Hazelnuts
35. Macadamia Nuts
36. Cashews
37. Pistachios
38. Chestnuts
39. Brazil Nuts
40. Pine Nuts

Seafood:
41. Smoked Salmon
42. Oysters
43. Shrimp
44. Crab Cakes
45. Lobster
46. Scallops
47. Calamari
48. Mussels
49. Tuna Sashimi
50. Caviar

Vegetables:
51. Roasted Butternut Squash
52. Brussels Sprouts
53. Caramelized Onions
54. Artichokes
55. Roasted Beets
56. Sweet Potatoes
57. Asparagus
58. Grilled Zucchini
59. Mushrooms
60. Roasted Red Peppers

Appetizers:
61. Bacon-Wrapped Dates
62. Stuffed Mushrooms
63. Deviled Eggs
64. Truffle Fries
65. Crab Stuffed Jalapeños
66. Spanakopita
67. Mini Quiches
68. Gougères
69. Crostini with Goat Cheese and Honey
70. Tomato Bruschetta

Main Courses:
71. Maple-Glazed Salmon
72. Pork Tenderloin with Apple Compote
73. Duck Confit
74. Chicken Liver Pâté
75. Honey Mustard Glazed Ham
76. Roast Turkey
77. Beef Tenderloin with Red Wine Reduction
78. Seared Scallops with Brown Butter
79. Grilled Lamb Chops
80. Osso Buco

Pasta and Rice:
81. Pumpkin Risotto
82. Butternut Squash Ravioli
83. Wild Mushroom Risotto
84. Truffle Mac 'n' Cheese
85. Shrimp Scampi
86. Lobster Pasta
87. Pesto Gnocchi
88. Seafood Paella
89. Sweet Potato Gnocchi
90. Lemon Butter Linguine

Salads:
91. Apple and Walnut Salad
92. Goat Cheese and Pear Salad
93. Spinach Salad with Bacon and Cranberries
94. Beetroot and Goat Cheese Salad
95. Caesar Salad
96. Arugula Salad with Prosciutto
97. Caprese Salad
98. Waldorf Salad
99. Grilled Peach Salad
100. Fig and Prosciutto

Contemporary Ice Cider Recipes Inspired by the Ancient Romans

In this culinary journey, we re-imagine Ancient Roman dishes, infusing them with the modern luxury of high-end ice cider. Witness the evolution of classics as we marry the wisdom of antiquity with the nuanced sweetness, complexity, and depth of ice cider. Each dish, carefully adapted, bridges the gap between tradition and contemporary indulgence.

1. *Mulsum* (Adapted with Ice Cider):
Experience the refreshing fusion of honey and ice cider, transforming the ancient Roman honeyed wine, *Mulsum*.

2. *Patina de Piris* (Pear Soufflé with Ice Cider Reduction):
Elevate the classic pear soufflé with a decadent ice cider reduction, adding a contemporary twist to this timeless dessert.

3. *Libum* (Honey and Cheese Cake with Ice Cider Glaze):
Witness the delicate marriage of honey and cheese cake adorned with a high-end ice cider glaze, harmonizing ancient and modern flavors.

4. *Conditum Paradoxum* (Spiced Wine with Ice Cider):
Immerse yourself in the paradoxical delight of spiced wine with a unique twist—ice cider replacing some of the wine.

5. *Ova Spongia ex Lacte* (Milk and Honey Sponge Cake with Ice Cider Infusion):
Explore the modern twist of a milk and honey sponge cake with an infusion of ice cider, enhancing its timeless simplicity.

6. *Gustum de Pruna* (Plum Pudding with Ice Cider Sauce):
Embrace the classic Roman plum pudding with a modern drizzle—sauce made from reduced ice cider—for a timeless yet contemporary dessert.

7. *Pullum Frontonianum* (Frontonian Chicken with Ice Cider Marinade):
Let the flavors of Frontonian Chicken soar with an ice cider-infused marinade, adding a succulent touch to this ancient dish.

8. *Dulcia Domestica* (Domestic Sweets with Ice Cider Glaze):
Indulge in Roman sweets adorned with a glaze made from reduced ice cider, marrying tradition with a touch of modern sophistication.

9. *Pernam* (Honey-Glazed Ham with Ice Cider):
Elevate the classic Roman honey-glazed ham by infusing it with the richness of high-end ice cider.

10. *Gustum de Cervisia* (Beer-Based Dish with Ice Cider):
Experience the fusion of brews as we reimagine beer-based dishes with the addition of ice cider, creating a contemporary culinary symphony.

Join us as we bridge the gap between ancient and modern, savoring the exquisite touch of ice cider in each bite. Cheers to a journey that transcends time and tantalizes the taste buds with the spirit of innovation and luxury.

Contemporary Ice Cider Recipes inspired by the Ancient Romans
1. Adapted Mulsum Recipe with Ice Cider: A Modern Elixir

Transport yourself to the ancient Roman era with a contemporary twist on the classic *Mulsum*. This adapted recipe replaces traditional wine with the luscious sweetness of ice cider, resulting in a refreshing elixir that seamlessly marries the flavors of honey, spices, and citrus. Prepare to embark on a journey through time as you indulge in this modern interpretation of a historic libation.

Ingredients:

- 1 bottle (750 ml) high-quality ice cider
- 1/2 cup honey (adjust to taste)
- 1 orange, sliced
- 1 lemon, sliced
- 2 cinnamon sticks
- 3-4 whole cloves
- Ice cubes (optional)
- Fresh mint leaves for garnish

Instructions:

1. Prepare Ingredients:
   Slice orange and lemon. Measure honey. Gather cinnamon sticks, cloves, and mint.

2. Warm Ice Cider:
   Pour ice cider into a saucepan. Warm gently. Avoid boiling. Dissolve honey.

3. Add Honey and Spices:
   Add honey. Stir until dissolved. Add cinnamon, cloves, and half of citrus slices. Simmer for 10-15 minutes.

4. Strain and Chill:
   Remove from heat. Strain to remove spices and fruit. Cool to room temperature. Chill in the refrigerator for at least two hours.

5. Serve:
   Fill glasses with ice. Pour chilled *Mulsum*. Garnish with remaining citrus slices and mint.

6. Enjoy:
   Sip and savor the modern *Mulsum* with ice cider—a refreshing blend of sweetness, warmth, and citrus notes. Share with friends or indulge in a moment of self-enjoyment. Cheers to a timeless beverage reimagined!

Contemporary Ice Cider Recipes inspired by the Ancient Romans

2. Patina de Piris (Pear Soufflé with Ice Cider Reduction)

Patina de Piris is a culinary enchantment that unfolds in layers of flavor and elegance. Ripe pears, caramelized and pureed, form the soul of a delicate soufflé batter, a marriage of fruity richness and ethereal lightness. As the soufflés rise to golden perfection, they are crowned with an ice cider reduction, a glossy elixir simmered from ice cider and honey, adding sweet complexity. Dusting each soufflé with powdered sugar completes the visual allure. Served immediately, this dessert is a symphony—a harmonious blend of caramelized pears and velvety ice cider reduction, creating a sensory experience that resonates on the palate with every sublime bite.

Ingredients:

- 2 ripe pears, peeled, cored, and diced
- 1 tablespoon unsalted butter
- 1/4 cup sugar
- 1 teaspoon lemon juice
- 3 large eggs, separated
- 1/4 cup ice cider
- 1/4 cup all-purpose flour
- Pinch of salt
- Powdered sugar for dusting

For the Ice Cider Reduction:

- 1 cup ice cider
- 2 tablespoons honey

Instructions:

1. Prep Oven & Ramekins:
   Preheat the oven to 375°F (190°C) and prep four ramekins with butter and sugar.

2. Caramelize Pears:
   Melt butter, cook diced pears with sugar and lemon juice until caramelized. Let it cool, then puree.

3. Ice Cider Glaze:
   Simmer ice cider and honey until syrupy. Set aside to cool.

4. Soufflé Batter:
   Whisk pear puree with egg yolks, flour, and a pinch of salt.

5. Whip Egg Whites:
   Whip egg whites to stiff peaks in a separate bowl.

6. Combine and Bake:
   Gently fold whipped egg whites into the pear mixture. Fill ramekins and bake for 15-18 minutes until golden.

7. Ice Cider Drizzle:
   Post-bake, drizzle soufflés with cooled ice cider glaze for enhanced sweetness.

8. Powdered Elegance:
   Dust with powdered sugar just before serving for an elegant touch.

9. Enjoy:
   Serve immediately for a luxurious experience—*Patina de Piris*, a pear soufflé with a touch of ice cider magic.

Contemporary Ice Cider Recipes inspired by the Ancient Romans

3. Libum (Honey and Cheese Cake with Ice Cider Glaze)

Experience a culinary journey with *Libum*, a divine honey and cheese cake elevated to new heights by a decadent ice cider glaze. The recipe begins with the timeless combination of honey and cheese, crafting a cake that embodies richness and sweetness.

What makes *Libum* exceptional is the finishing touch—a reduction of ice cider transformed into a glaze. This velvety elixir, with its sweet and nuanced notes, cascades over the cake, imparting an additional layer of depth and complexity. Each slice of *Libum* is a celebration of tradition and innovation—a perfect union of ancient flavors and modern refinement, making it a dessert that transcends the ordinary and delights the palate with every sumptuous bite.

Ingredients:

- 1 cup ricotta cheese
- 1/4 cup honey
- 1 egg
- 1 cup all-purpose flour
- Pinch of salt

For the Ice Cider Glaze:

- 1/2 cup ice cider
- 2 tablespoons honey

Instructions:

1. Preheat the oven to 375°F (190°C) and grease a baking dish.

2. In a mixing bowl, combine ricotta cheese, honey, egg, flour, and a pinch of salt. Mix until well combined.

3. Form the mixture into small cakes and place them on the greased baking dish.

4. Bake for 20-25 minutes or until golden brown.

5. While the cakes cool, prepare the ice cider glaze. In a saucepan, combine ice cider and honey. Simmer until it thickens into a glaze.

6. Drizzle the ice cider glaze over the cooled honey and cheese cakes.

7. Allow the glaze to set for a few minutes, then serve and enjoy your delightful *Libum*—a perfect harmony of honey, cheese, and ice cider.

Contemporary Ice Cider Recipes inspired by the Ancient Romans
4. Conditum Paradoxum (Spiced Wine with Ice Cider)

Conditum Paradoxum, a classic spiced wine, takes an intriguing turn with the infusion of ice cider—a marriage of tradition and innovation that brings forth a delightful paradox for the palate. In this captivating concoction, the deep richness of red wine blends with the subtle sweetness of ice cider, creating a harmonious symphony of flavors.

The fragrance of cinnamon, cloves, and a hint of pepper infuse the air as the concoction gently simmers, allowing the spices to intertwine with the velvety notes of honey and sugar. The addition of ice cider introduces a sweet twist, elevating the warmth of the spiced wine to a new dimension. Strained for a seamless texture, this beverage invites you to savor the paradox—a celebration of time-honored flavors woven together with a contemporary touch.

Serve it warm, perhaps garnished with a cinnamon stick or a twist of orange peel, and embark on a journey that transcends the ordinary, where the familiar comforts of spiced wine are met with the sweet surprise of ice cider—an enchanting and paradoxical delight for the senses.

Ingredients:

- 1 bottle red wine
- 1/2 cup honey
- 1/4 cup sugar
- 1 cinnamon stick
- 3 whole cloves
- 1 pinch ground pepper
- 1/2 cup ice cider (replace a portion of the wine)

Instructions:

1. Combine Ingredients:
   In a saucepan, combine red wine, honey, sugar, cinnamon stick, cloves, and ground pepper. Add a sweet twist by incorporating 1/2 cup of ice cider, replacing a portion of the wine.

2. Simmer and Infuse:
   Heat the mixture over medium-low heat, allowing the flavors to meld. Simmer gently; do not boil. Let the spices infuse into the concoction.

3. Strain and Serve:
   Once the fragrance fills the air, remove the spices by straining the spiced wine with ice cider. This step ensures a smooth and flavorful beverage.

4. Warm and Enjoy:
   Warm the spiced drink and serve in heat-resistant glasses. The addition of ice cider introduces a delightful sweetness, elevating the traditional *Conditum Paradoxum* into a uniquely spiced wine with a sweet twist.

5. Garnish (Optional):
   Garnish with a cinnamon stick or orange peel if desired. Sip and savor the warmth of spiced wine with the enhanced sweetness and flavor courtesy of the ice cider infusion—a delightful paradox that tantalizes the taste buds.

Contemporary Ice Cider Recipes inspired by the Ancient Romans

5. Ova Spongia ex Lacte (Milk and Honey Sponge Cake with Ice Cider Infusion)

Indulge in the harmonious blend of tradition and innovation with Ova *Spongia ex Lacte*—a luscious Milk and Honey Sponge Cake elevated by an ice cider infusion. This delicacy marries the timeless sweetness of honey and milk with the modern twist of ice cider, resulting in a cake that's light, moist, and brimming with delightful nuances.

Ingredients:

- 2 cups all-purpose flour
- 1 cup milk
- 1/2 cup honey
- 1/2 cup ice cider
- 1/2 cup unsalted butter, melted
- 3 large eggs
- 1 tablespoon baking powder
- Pinch of salt

Instructions:

1. Preheat oven to 350°F (175°C) and grease a cake pan.

2. In a bowl, whisk together flour, baking powder, and salt.

3. In another bowl, beat eggs and gradually add honey, melted butter, and milk. Mix until smooth.

4. Combine the wet and dry ingredients, then fold in the ice cider gently.

5. Pour the batter into the prepared pan and bake for 25-30 minutes or until a toothpick comes out clean.

6. Let the cake cool, slice, and savor the exquisite fusion of flavors—a symphony of milk, honey, and the nuanced sweetness of ice cider.

Contemporary Ice Cider Recipes inspired by the Ancient Romans
6. Gustum de Pruna (Plum Pudding with Ice Cider Sauce)

Savor the rich indulgence of *Gustum de Pruna*—a Plum Pudding elevated to new heights by the velvety embrace of an Ice Cider Sauce. This classic dessert, infused with the essence of ripe plums and crowned with a luscious ice cider sauce, presents a symphony of flavors that dances on the palate.

Ingredients:

- 2 cups chopped plums
- 1 cup all-purpose flour
- 1 cup breadcrumbs
- 1 cup brown sugar
- 1 cup suet or vegetarian suet
- 1 cup ice cider
- 1/2 cup chopped almonds
- 1/2 cup raisins
- 1 teaspoon ground cinnamon
- 1 teaspoon ground nutmeg
- 1 teaspoon baking soda
- Pinch of salt

For the Ice Cider Sauce:

- 1/2 cup ice cider
- 1/4 cup butter
- 1/4 cup brown sugar

Instructions:

1. Preheat oven to 350°F (175°C) and grease a pudding mold.

2. In a large bowl, combine chopped plums, flour, breadcrumbs, brown sugar, suet, ice cider, almonds, raisins, cinnamon, nutmeg, baking soda, and a pinch of salt. Mix thoroughly.

3. Pour the mixture into the prepared mold and cover with a lid or foil.

4. Steam the pudding for 2 to 3 hours until it's firm and cooked through.

5. For the Ice Cider Sauce: In a saucepan, combine ice cider, butter, and brown sugar. Simmer until it forms a smooth sauce.

6. Once the pudding is done, remove it from the mold and serve warm with a generous drizzle of the Ice Cider Sauce.

7. Slice, serve, and relish the exquisite *Gustum de Pruna*—a Plum Pudding with Ice Cider Sauce that promises to transport your taste buds to a realm of sweet sophistication.

Contemporary Ice Cider Recipes inspired by the Ancient Romans

7. Pullum Frontonianum (Frontonian Chicken with Ice Cider Marinade)

Embark on a culinary journey with *Pullum Frontonianum*—a succulent Frontonian Chicken elevated to greatness through a tantalizing Ice Cider Marinade. This dish is a celebration of flavors inspired by ancient Frontonian traditions, where the natural sweetness and complexity of ice cider intermingle with the savory essence of chicken, creating a symphony on the taste buds.

Ingredients:

- 4 boneless, skinless chicken breasts
- 1 cup ice cider
- 1/4 cup olive oil
- 2 cloves garlic, minced
- 2 tablespoons honey
- 1 tablespoon Dijon mustard
- 1 teaspoon dried thyme
- 1 teaspoon paprika
- Salt and pepper to taste
- Fresh parsley for garnish

Instructions:

1. In a bowl, whisk together ice cider, olive oil, minced garlic, honey, Dijon mustard, dried thyme, paprika, salt, and pepper to create the marinade.

2. Place chicken breasts in a resealable plastic bag or a shallow dish and pour the ice cider marinade over them.

3. Ensure chicken is well-coated, seal the bag or cover the dish, and refrigerate for at least 2 hours, or preferably overnight, to let the flavors infuse.

4. Preheat the grill or oven to medium-high heat.

5. Remove the chicken from the marinade, allowing excess to drip off.

6. Grill or bake the chicken until cooked through, approximately 6-8 minutes per side, depending on thickness.

7. Garnish with fresh parsley and serve the *Pullum Frontonianum* hot, showcasing the perfect union of tender chicken and the distinctive flavors of the Ice Cider Marinade.

8. Relish in the exquisite blend of savory and sweet, appreciating the ancient-inspired culinary triumph that is *Pullum Frontonianum*—a dish that bridges the past and present with each delectable bite.

Contemporary Ice Cider Recipes inspired by the Ancient Romans
8. Dulcia Domestica (Domestic Sweets with Ice Cider Glaze)

Impress your diners with this delightful journey with *Dulcia Domestica*—homemade sweets elevated to perfection with an enchanting Ice Cider Glaze. This collection of domestic treats promises to infuse your kitchen with the sweet aroma of tradition and innovation, where the golden essence of ice cider adds a touch of magic to every delectable bite.

Ingredients:

For the Sweets:

- 2 cups all-purpose flour
- 1 cup sugar
- 1/2 cup unsalted butter, softened
- 2 eggs
- 1 teaspoon vanilla extract
- 1/2 cup milk
- 1 tablespoon baking powder
- Pinch of salt

For the Ice Cider Glaze:

- 1 cup powdered sugar
- 1/4 cup ice cider
- 1/2 teaspoon vanilla extract

Instructions:

1. Preheat the oven to 350°F (175°C) and prepare a baking sheet with parchment paper.

2. In a mixing bowl, cream together softened butter and sugar until light and fluffy. Add eggs one at a time, beating well after each addition. Stir in vanilla extract.

3. In a separate bowl, whisk together flour, baking powder, and a pinch of salt.

4. Gradually add the dry ingredients to the wet ingredients, alternating with milk. Mix until just combined.

5. Drop spoonfuls of batter onto the prepared baking sheet, leaving space between each.

6. Bake for 10-12 minutes or until the edges are golden brown. Allow the sweets to cool.

7. For the Ice Cider Glaze, whisk together powdered sugar, ice cider, and vanilla extract until smooth.

8. Once the sweets have cooled, drizzle the Ice Cider Glaze over the top.

9. Allow the glaze to set, and then indulge in *Dulcia Domestica*—a symphony of homemade sweets adorned with the exquisite touch of an ice cider glaze, blending tradition and innovation in every delightful bite.

Contemporary Ice Cider Recipes inspired by the Ancient Romans
9. Pernam (Honey-Glazed Ham with Ice Cider)

Immerse yourself in a culinary spectacle with *Pernam*—an exquisite Honey-Glazed Ham elevated to extraordinary heights with the addition of a luscious Ice Cider glaze. This timeless dish, inspired by ancient flavors, marries the succulence of honey-glazed ham with the nuanced sweetness and complexity of ice cider, resulting in a symphony of taste and aroma that promises to enchant your table.

Ingredients:

- 1 bone-in ham, about 8-10 pounds
- 1 cup ice cider
- 1/2 cup honey
- 1/4 cup Dijon mustard
- 1/4 cup brown sugar
- 1 teaspoon ground cloves
- 1 teaspoon ground cinnamon
- 1/2 teaspoon ground nutmeg
- Salt and pepper to taste

Instructions:

1. Preheat the oven to 325°F (163°C).

2. Place the ham in a roasting pan, fat side up. Score the surface with diagonal cuts, creating a diamond pattern.

3. In a bowl, whisk together ice cider, honey, Dijon mustard, brown sugar, ground cloves, ground cinnamon, ground nutmeg, salt, and pepper to create the glaze.

4. Generously brush the ham with the ice cider glaze, ensuring it seeps into the scored cuts.

5. Cover the ham with aluminum foil and bake for approximately 15-20 minutes per pound, or until the internal temperature reaches 140°F (60°C).

6. During the last 30 minutes of baking, baste the ham with the ice cider glaze every 10 minutes to build a flavorful, caramelized crust.

7. Once done, remove the ham from the oven and let it rest for 15 minutes before carving.

8. Serve the *Pernam* with the remaining ice cider glaze on the side, allowing your guests to savor the perfect harmony of honey-glazed ham enriched by the subtle sweetness and depth of the ice cider—a feast that captures the essence of ancient culinary wisdom.

Contemporary Ice Cider Recipes inspired by the Ancient Romans
10. Gustum de Cervisia (Beer-Based Dish with Ice Cider)

Embark on a flavorful journey with *Gustum de Cervisia*—a beer-based dish that reaches new heights with the infusion of Ice Cider. This culinary creation brings together the robust essence of beer with the nuanced sweetness and complexity of ice cider, resulting in a harmonious blend that tantalizes the taste buds.

Ingredients:

- 2 pounds beef stew meat, cubed
- 2 tablespoons olive oil
- 1 onion, diced
- 2 carrots, sliced
- 2 cloves garlic, minced
- 2 cups dark beer
- 1 cup ice cider
- 1 cup beef broth
- 2 tablespoons tomato paste
- 1 tablespoon Worcestershire sauce
- 1 teaspoon dried thyme
- Salt and pepper to taste
- 2 tablespoons all-purpose flour (for thickening)

Instructions:

1. In a large pot or Dutch oven, heat olive oil over medium-high heat. Brown the beef stew meat in batches, ensuring each piece is seared on all sides. Remove and set aside.

2. In the same pot, sauté diced onion, sliced carrots, and minced garlic until softened.

3. Return the seared beef to the pot. Add dark beer, ice cider, beef broth, tomato paste, Worcestershire sauce, dried thyme, salt, and pepper. Bring to a boil.

4. Reduce the heat to low, cover, and simmer for 2 to 2.5 hours or until the beef is tender.

5. In a small bowl, mix flour with a bit of water to create a smooth paste. Stir the flour paste into the stew to thicken the broth.

6. Continue simmering for an additional 15-20 minutes until the stew reaches your desired thickness.

7. Adjust seasoning if necessary and serve the *Gustum de Cervisia* hot. The infusion of ice cider adds a sweet complexity to the rich, beer-infused broth, creating a dish that is both comforting and uniquely flavorful.

8. Pair with your favorite bread or mashed potatoes to soak up the delicious broth, and savor the fusion of beer and ice cider in this hearty and satisfying dish.

Contemporary Ice Cider Recipes inspired by the Medieval Culinary Traditions

Journey through the annals of medieval gastronomy with a contemporary twist as we re-imagine classic recipes infused with the richness of high-end ice cider. In this culinary adventure, we seamlessly blend the timeless charm of medieval flavors with the nuanced sweetness, complexity, and depth that ice cider imparts. Join us in this fusion of eras, where tradition meets modern opulence, creating a symphony of taste that transcends time.

1. Mead-Braised Chicken with Ice Cider Glaze:
Breathe new life into medieval cuisine by braising chicken in mead and finishing it with an exquisite ice cider glaze—a sweet and savory fusion.

2. Honeyed Roasted Vegetables with Ice Cider Drizzle:
Elevate roasted vegetables with a medieval touch, drizzled with a reduction of ice cider, harmonizing the old-world honeyed flavors with contemporary luxury.

3. Barley and Ice Cider Soup:
Experience the comforting warmth of medieval barley soup, enhanced by the subtle sweetness of ice cider—a simple yet sophisticated twist.

4. Medieval Meat Pie with Ice Cider Infused Filling:
Indulge in a medieval meat pie, now elevated with an infusion of ice cider, seamlessly blending tradition with modern flair.

5. Pottage of Lentils with Ice Cider Reduction:
Transform a bowl of lentil pottage into a culinary masterpiece with a reduction of ice cider, adding depth to this medieval classic.

6. Spiced Ice Cider Nuts:
Roasted mixed nuts, kissed with medieval spices and an ice cider glaze, create a sensory delight that bridges eras.

7. Ale and Ice Cider Bread:
Enrich a traditional medieval ale bread recipe with the contemporary twist of ice cider, infusing the bread with a unique and modern flavor.

8. Apple and Ice Cider Stew:
Immerse yourself in a sweet and savory stew, where medieval influences meet modern refinement, with ice cider as the base liquid.

9. Medieval-Inspired Ice Cider Tarts:
Delight in small tarts filled with fruits and nuts, sweetened with ice cider, creating a harmonious blend of medieval simplicity and contemporary opulence.

10. Ice Cider Wassail:
Embrace the festive spirit of medieval times with a contemporary ice cider wassail, blending warm spices with the exquisite flavor of ice cider.

Contemporary Ice Cider Recipes inspired by the Medieval Culinary Traditions
1. Mead-Braised Chicken with Ice Cider Glaze

Elevate your culinary experience with this medieval-inspired Mead-Braised Chicken, where succulent chicken is bathed in a mead-infused braise and crowned with a decadent ice cider glaze. The result is a harmonious blend of sweet and savory notes that transport your taste buds to a feast fit for royalty.

Ingredients:

- 4 bone-in, skin-on chicken thighs
- Salt and pepper to taste
- 1 cup mead
- 1/2 cup chicken broth
- 2 tablespoons olive oil
- 1/4 cup high-end ice cider
- 2 tablespoons honey
- Fresh thyme for garnish

Instructions:

1. Season chicken thighs with salt and pepper.

2. In a pan, heat olive oil over medium-high heat. Sear chicken until golden brown on both sides.

3. Pour in mead and chicken broth, bringing it to a simmer. Cover and let it braise for 25-30 minutes or until chicken is cooked through.

4. In a separate saucepan, combine ice cider and honey. Simmer until it thickens into a glaze.

5. Brush the ice cider glaze over the braised chicken, ensuring it coats each piece. Allow it to caramelize for a few minutes.

6. Garnish with fresh thyme and serve hot. Indulge in the Mead-Braised Chicken with Ice Cider Glaze—a culinary masterpiece that marries medieval charm with modern luxury.

Contemporary Ice Cider Recipes inspired by the Medieval Culinary Traditions

2. Honeyed Roasted Vegetables with Ice Cider Drizzle

Transport your palate to medieval banquets with this exquisite dish of Honeyed Roasted Vegetables. A symphony of root vegetables, honey, and medieval spices, roasted to perfection and crowned with a luxurious ice cider reduction, creates a culinary masterpiece that seamlessly blends antiquity with contemporary indulgence.

Ingredients:

- Assorted root vegetables (carrots, parsnips, turnips), peeled and chopped
- 2 tablespoons olive oil
- Salt and pepper to taste
- 1/4 cup honey
- 1/4 cup high-end ice cider
- Medieval spice blend (cinnamon, nutmeg, cloves)

Instructions:

1. Preheat your oven to 400°F (200°C).

2. In a large bowl, toss the chopped root vegetables with olive oil, salt, and pepper until evenly coated.

3. Spread the vegetables on a baking sheet in a single layer. Roast in the preheated oven for 25-30 minutes or until they are golden and caramelized.

4. In a small saucepan, combine honey, ice cider, and a pinch of the medieval spice blend. Simmer over low heat until it forms a rich reduction.

5. Drizzle the ice cider reduction over the roasted vegetables, ensuring each piece is coated.

6. Toss the vegetables gently to evenly distribute the honeyed ice cider glaze.

7. Transfer to a serving platter, sprinkle with a bit more of the medieval spice blend for an extra touch, and serve immediately.

8. Relish in the Honeyed Roasted Vegetables with Ice Cider Drizzle—a dish that pays homage to medieval feasts while embracing the luxury of contemporary flavor.

Contemporary Ice Cider Recipes inspired by the Medieval Culinary Traditions
3. Barley and Ice Cider Soup

Embark on a journey through time with this medieval-inspired Barley and Ice Cider Soup. A robust fusion of barley, vegetables, and savory broth, elevated by the subtle sweetness of high-end ice cider. This hearty dish offers a taste of antiquity with a contemporary twist, warming both body and soul.

Ingredients:

- 1 cup pearl barley
- 1 onion, finely chopped
- 2 carrots, diced
- 2 celery stalks, sliced
- 3 cloves garlic, minced
- 6 cups chicken or vegetable broth
- 1/2 cup high-end ice cider
- Salt and pepper to taste
- Fresh herbs for garnish (parsley, thyme)

Instructions:

1. In a large pot, sauté chopped onion, carrots, celery, and garlic until softened.

2. Add pearl barley to the pot and stir to coat with the vegetables.

3. Pour in the chicken or vegetable broth, bringing the mixture to a gentle boil.

4. Reduce heat to low, cover, and simmer for about 45 minutes or until the barley is tender.

5. Stir in high-end ice cider, allowing it to impart its subtle sweetness to the soup. Simmer for an additional 10 minutes.

6. Season the soup with salt and pepper to taste.

7. Ladle the Barley and Ice Cider Soup into bowls, garnishing with fresh herbs for an extra layer of flavor.

8. Serve hot and savor the medieval-inspired elixir that combines the wholesome richness of barley with the contemporary touch of high-quality ice cider.

Contemporary Ice Cider Recipes inspired by the Medieval Culinary Traditions
4. Medieval Meat Pie with Ice Cider Infused Filling

Embark on a culinary odyssey with this Medieval Meat Pie, where rich, savory flavors of a hearty filling meet the luxurious touch of ice cider infusion. Encased in a golden crust, this timeless dish transports your taste buds to the medieval banquet halls, blending tradition with a contemporary twist.

Ingredients:

For the Filling:
- 1 lb ground meat (beef, pork, or a mix)
- 1 onion, finely chopped
- 2 cloves garlic, minced
- 1/2 cup high-end ice cider
- 2 tablespoons flour
- Salt and pepper to taste
- Medieval spice blend (rosemary, thyme, sage)

For the Pie Crust:
- 2 1/2 cups all-purpose flour
- 1 cup cold butter, cubed
- 1/4 cup ice water
- 1 teaspoon salt

Instructions:

For the Filling:

1. In a skillet, sauté chopped onion and minced garlic until softened.

2. Add ground meat to the skillet, cooking until browned. Drain excess fat.

3. Sprinkle flour over the meat, stirring to coat evenly.

4. Pour in high-end ice cider, allowing it to deglaze the pan. Add the medieval spice blend, salt, and pepper. Simmer until the liquid thickens.

For the Pie Crust:

1. In a food processor, pulse flour and cold, cubed butter until it resembles coarse crumbs.

2. Add ice water, one tablespoon at a time, pulsing until the dough comes together.

3. Divide the dough in half, shape into discs, and refrigerate for at least 30 minutes.

Assembling the Pie:

1. Preheat your oven to 375°F (190°C).

2. Roll out one disc of the pie crust and line a pie dish.

3. Fill the crust with the ice cider-infused meat filling.

4. Roll out the second disc and place it over the filling. Seal and crimp the edges.

5. Make a few slits in the top crust for ventilation.

6. Bake in the preheated oven for 40-45 minutes or until the crust is golden brown.

7. Allow the Medieval Meat Pie to cool slightly before slicing and savoring the marriage of medieval flavors and contemporary indulgence.

Contemporary Ice Cider Recipes inspired by the Medieval Culinary Traditions
5. Pottage of Lentils with Ice Cider Reduction

Delight in the simplicity of a medieval-inspired Pottage of Lentils, where humble lentils are transformed into a rich and flavorful dish. Elevating tradition, a velvety ice cider reduction drizzle adds a touch of sophistication to this hearty pottage, creating a culinary masterpiece that transcends time.

Ingredients:

- 1 cup dried lentils, rinsed and drained
- 1 onion, finely chopped
- 2 carrots, diced
- 2 celery stalks, sliced
- 3 cloves garlic, minced
- 6 cups vegetable broth
- 1/2 cup high-end ice cider
- Salt and pepper to taste
- Fresh parsley for garnish

Instructions:

1. In a large pot, sauté chopped onion, carrots, celery, and garlic until softened.

2. Add dried lentils to the pot and stir to combine with the vegetables.

3. Pour in vegetable broth, bringing the mixture to a gentle boil.

4. Reduce heat to low, cover, and simmer for about 25-30 minutes or until the lentils are tender.

5. Stir in high-end ice cider, allowing it to impart a subtle sweetness to the pottage. Simmer for an additional 10 minutes.

6. Season the pottage with salt and pepper to taste.

7. Ladle the Pottage of Lentils into bowls, garnishing with fresh parsley for a burst of color and freshness.

8. Serve hot and relish in the comforting harmony of medieval flavors enriched by the contemporary touch of high-quality ice cider.

Contemporary Ice Cider Recipes inspired by the Medieval Culinary Traditions

6. Spiced Ice Cider Nuts

Embark on a sensory journey with these Spiced Ice Cider Nuts—a medieval-inspired treat elevated by contemporary luxury. Mixed nuts, coated in a blend of medieval spices, are roasted to perfection and finished with a glaze made from high-end ice cider. This delectable fusion of flavors is a testament to the timeless appeal of indulgence.

Ingredients:

- 2 cups mixed nuts (almonds, walnuts, pecans)
- 1/4 cup high-end ice cider
- 2 tablespoons honey
- 1 teaspoon medieval spice blend (cinnamon, nutmeg, cloves)
- 1/2 teaspoon salt

Instructions:

1. Preheat your oven to 350°F (175°C).

2. In a bowl, combine mixed nuts with high-end ice cider, ensuring they are well-coated.

3. Spread the nuts on a baking sheet lined with parchment paper.

4. In a small saucepan, heat honey over low heat until it becomes liquid. Add the medieval spice blend and salt, stirring until well combined.

5. Drizzle the spiced honey mixture over the nuts on the baking sheet.

6. Toss the nuts to ensure an even coating of the spiced honey mixture.

7. Roast in the preheated oven for 15-20 minutes, stirring halfway through, or until the nuts are golden and fragrant.

8. Remove from the oven and let the nuts cool completely on the baking sheet.

9. Once cooled, break apart any clusters and transfer to a serving bowl.

10. Indulge in the Spiced Ice Cider Nuts—a medieval-inspired delight that marries the richness of nuts with the exquisite touch of high-quality ice cider.

Contemporary Ice Cider Recipes inspired by the Medieval Culinary Traditions

7. Ale and Ice Cider Bread

Transport your taste buds to the medieval hearths with this Ale and Ice Cider Bread—a rustic masterpiece that harmonizes the robust essence of ale with the nuanced sweetness of high-end ice cider. This loaf, with its hearty crust and flavorful crumb, embodies the timeless spirit of breaking bread in a medieval feast.

Ingredients:

- 3 cups all-purpose flour
- 1 cup ale (preferably a dark ale)
- 1/2 cup high-end ice cider
- 1 packet (2 1/4 teaspoons) active dry yeast
- 1 tablespoon honey
- 1 teaspoon salt
- 2 tablespoons olive oil

Instructions:

1. In a small bowl, combine ale and ice cider. Warm the mixture slightly if it's too cold.

2. Dissolve honey in the ale and ice cider mixture. Sprinkle active dry yeast over the liquid and let it sit for about 5 minutes until foamy.

3. In a large mixing bowl, combine flour and salt.

4. Make a well in the center of the flour mixture and pour in the yeast mixture.

5. Gradually incorporate the flour into the liquid, stirring until a dough forms.

6. Turn the dough out onto a floured surface and knead for about 8-10 minutes, or until the dough becomes smooth and elastic.

7. Place the dough in a lightly oiled bowl, cover with a damp cloth, and let it rise in a warm place for 1-2 hours, or until doubled in size.

8. Preheat your oven to 375°F (190°C).

9. Punch down the risen dough and shape it into a round loaf. Place the loaf on a baking sheet lined with parchment paper.

10. Let the shaped dough rise for an additional 30-45 minutes.

11. Brush the loaf with olive oil before baking.

12. Bake in the preheated oven for 30-35 minutes, or until the bread is golden brown and sounds hollow when tapped on the bottom.

13. Allow the Ale and Ice Cider Bread to cool before slicing. Serve and savor the medieval essence of this hearty loaf.

Contemporary Ice Cider Recipes inspired by the Medieval Culinary Traditions
8. Apple and Ice Cider Stew

Embark on a culinary journey to medieval kitchens with this Apple and Ice Cider Stew—a dish that seamlessly blends the sweetness of apples with the nuanced depth of high-end ice cider. Slow-cooked to perfection, this hearty stew captures the essence of medieval comfort, marrying tradition with a touch of contemporary luxury.

Ingredients:

- 4 apples, peeled, cored, and sliced
- 1 lb pork or chicken, cubed
- 1 onion, finely chopped
- 2 carrots, diced
- 2 cloves garlic, minced
- 1/2 cup high-end ice cider
- 1 cup chicken or vegetable broth
- 2 tablespoons olive oil
- 1 teaspoon dried thyme
- Salt and pepper to taste

Instructions:

1. In a large pot, heat olive oil over medium heat. Add cubed meat and brown on all sides.

2. Add chopped onion and minced garlic to the pot, sautéing until softened.

3. Pour in high-end ice cider, deglazing the pot and scraping up any flavorful bits.

4. Add sliced apples, diced carrots, and dried thyme to the pot. Stir to combine.

5. Pour in chicken or vegetable broth, ensuring the ingredients are well-submerged.

6. Season the stew with salt and pepper to taste. Bring the mixture to a gentle boil.

7. Reduce the heat to low, cover the pot, and simmer for 45 minutes to 1 hour, or until the meat is tender.

8. Taste and adjust the seasoning if needed.

9. Serve the Apple and Ice Cider Stew hot, allowing the medieval-inspired flavors to delight your senses. Pair with crusty bread for an authentic experience.

Contemporary Ice Cider Recipes inspired by the Medieval Culinary Traditions

9. Medieval-Inspired Ice Cider Tarts

Step into the past with these Medieval-Inspired Ice Cider Tarts—a delectable fusion of medieval charm and contemporary luxury. These petite tarts are filled with a mixture of fruits and nuts, sweetened to perfection with the golden touch of high-end ice cider. Indulge in each bite as you experience the sweetness of tradition with a modern twist.

Ingredients:

For the Tart Crust:
- 2 cups all-purpose flour
- 1/2 cup unsalted butter, chilled and cubed
- 1/4 cup sugar
- 1/4 cup ice water

For the Filling:
- 1 cup mixed dried fruits (figs, dates, raisins)
- 1/2 cup chopped nuts (almonds, walnuts)
- 1/2 cup high-end ice cider
- 2 tablespoons honey
- 1/2 teaspoon medieval spice blend (cinnamon, nutmeg)

Instructions:

For the Tart Crust:

1. In a food processor, pulse flour, sugar, and chilled butter until the mixture resembles coarse crumbs.

2. Add ice water gradually, pulsing until the dough comes together.

3. Shape the dough into a disk, wrap in plastic wrap, and refrigerate for at least 30 minutes.

4. Preheat your oven to 375°F (190°C).

5. Roll out the chilled dough and line tart pans. Prick the bottom of the crust with a fork.

6. Blind bake the tart crusts for 10-12 minutes or until lightly golden. Remove from the oven and let them cool.

For the Filling:

1. In a saucepan, combine high-end ice cider, honey, and medieval spice blend. Simmer over low heat until it forms a syrupy reduction.

2. In a bowl, mix dried fruits and chopped nuts. Pour the ice cider reduction over the mixture and stir until well coated.

Assembling the Tarts:

1. Spoon the fruit and nut mixture into the pre-baked tart crusts.

2. Bake in the preheated oven for an additional 15-18 minutes or until the filling is set.

3. Allow the tarts to cool completely before serving.

4. Enjoy the Medieval-Inspired Ice Cider Tarts—a delightful blend of history and modernity in every sweet, golden bite.

Contemporary Ice Cider Recipes inspired by the Medieval Culinary Traditions

10. Ice Cider Wassail

Celebrate the spirit of medieval merriment with this Ice Cider Wassail—a contemporary twist on the classic festive drink. Immerse yourself in the warmth of spices and the exquisite flavor of high-end ice cider, creating a beverage that transcends time. Raise your cup in a joyous wassail, toasting to the richness of tradition blended with the luxury of modern indulgence.

Ingredients:

- 1 quart (4 cups) apple cider
- 1 cup high-end ice cider
- 1 orange, sliced
- 1 lemon, sliced
- 6 cloves
- 2 cinnamon sticks
- 1/2 teaspoon ground nutmeg
- 1/4 cup honey
- 1 cup dark rum (optional)
- Sliced apples and cinnamon sticks for garnish

Instructions:

1. In a large pot, combine apple cider, high-end ice cider, orange slices, lemon slices, cloves, cinnamon sticks, and ground nutmeg.

2. Bring the mixture to a gentle simmer over medium heat. Do not let it boil.

3. Stir in honey, allowing it to dissolve into the wassail.

4. If adding rum, pour it into the wassail and stir to combine.

5. Let the wassail simmer for 15-20 minutes, allowing the flavors to meld.

6. Strain the wassail to remove the fruit slices and spices.

7. Pour the warm Ice Cider Wassail into mugs.

8. Garnish each mug with sliced apples and a cinnamon stick.

9. Raise your mug in a festive toast, sipping and savoring the delightful blend of spices and high-end ice cider. Enjoy the warmth and camaraderie of a medieval-inspired wassail!

Contemporary Ice Cider Recipes inspired by the Renaissance Culinary Traditions

In this section, we delve into the opulence of the Renaissance era, re-imagining classic recipes with the addition of the exquisite elixir–ice cider. Why bring such a beautiful, elegant, and expensive ingredient into these historic dishes? The answer lies in the desire to elevate these timeless recipes, marrying tradition with contemporary indulgence.

Ice cider, with its nuanced sweetness and complexity, becomes a culinary companion in this journey through Renaissance-inspired gastronomy. As you explore the following recipes, each one carefully curated to blend the richness of history with the modern luxury of ice cider, you embark on a flavorful expedition that transcends the boundaries of time.

1. **Pottage of Fruits with Ice Cider Reduction:** - A pottage of mixed fruits finished with a reduction of ice cider–a sweet and tangy glaze that transforms tradition into indulgence.

2. **Roast Game Hen with Ice Cider Marinade:** - Marinated in a mixture that includes ice cider, the game hen is roasted to succulent perfection–a dish that speaks of both opulence and flavor.

3. **Saffron Rice Pudding with Ice Cider Soaked Raisins:** - Ice cider-soaked raisins elevate saffron-infused rice pudding, creating a luxurious dessert fit for Renaissance royalty.

4. **Renaissance Chicken and Leek Pie with Ice Cider Gravy:** - Ice cider incorporated into the gravy of a savory chicken and leek pie–a harmonious marriage of sweet and savory.

5. **Barley and Ice Cider Ale:** - A traditional barley ale takes on a sweet and refreshing twist with the addition of ice cider–an elixir to elevate the ale experience.

6. **Honeyed Carrots with Ice Cider Glaze:** - Carrots glazed with honey and finished with a reduction of ice cider–a side dish bursting with layered flavors.

7. **Roasted Quail with Ice Cider Fig Compote:** - Roasted quail served with a fig compote sweetened with ice cider–a dish that captures the essence of Renaissance indulgence.

8. **Renaissance-Inspired Ice Cider Tiramisu:** - Ladyfingers infused with ice cider transform the classic tiramisu into a Renaissance-inspired delight–a dessert fit for the nobility.

9. **Pork and Apple Ice Cider Stew:** - A hearty pork stew with apples, vegetables, and a base of ice cider–an ode to the comforting richness of Renaissance cuisine.

10. **Renaissance Apple Tart with Ice Cider Glaze:** - An apple tart finished with a glaze made from reduced ice cider–a delicious dessert that bridges the gap between history and modernity.

Contemporary Ice Cider Recipes inspired by the Renaissance Culinary Traditions
1. Pottage of Fruits with Ice Cider Reduction

Pottage, a staple of Renaissance cuisine, was a pot-based dish that often included a mixture of meats, vegetables, and fruits. It was a versatile and hearty option enjoyed by both the nobility and commoners. Our adaptation focuses on the indulgent side of Renaissance dining, featuring a rich array of fruits complemented by the luxurious touch of ice cider.

Ingredients:

- 4 cups mixed fruits (such as apples, pears, berries)
- 1/2 cup high-end ice cider
- 2 tablespoons honey
- Pinch of cinnamon (optional)
- Mint leaves for garnish

Instructions:

1. In a pot, combine mixed fruits and high-end ice cider.

2. Bring the mixture to a gentle simmer over medium heat.

3. Stir in honey, ensuring it dissolves into the simmering fruits.

4. Let the fruits simmer for 10-15 minutes or until they are softened.

5. Optionally, add a pinch of cinnamon for a hint of warmth.

6. Remove from heat and let it cool slightly.

7. Serve the Pottage of Fruits in bowls, drizzling each portion with the ice cider reduction.

8. Garnish with fresh mint leaves for a touch of vibrancy.

9. Indulge in this Renaissance-inspired treat—a celebration of historical flavors enhanced by the contemporary luxury of ice cider.

Contemporary Ice Cider Recipes inspired by the Renaissance Culinary Traditions
2. Roast Game Hen with Ice Cider Marinade

Game hens were prized in Renaissance times for their delicate size and flavorful meat. Roasting, a common cooking method of the era, enhanced the natural richness of the poultry. Our adaptation introduces the luxurious twist of an ice cider marinade, elevating this classic dish to new heights.

Ingredients:

- 2 game hens, cleaned and patted dry
- 1/2 cup high-end ice cider
- 2 tablespoons olive oil
- 2 cloves garlic, minced
- 1 teaspoon dried thyme
- Salt and black pepper to taste
- Fresh herbs for garnish (rosemary, thyme)

Instructions:

1. Preheat your oven to 375°F (190°C).

2. In a bowl, whisk together high-end ice cider, olive oil, minced garlic, dried thyme, salt, and black pepper.

3. Place the game hens in a marinating dish and pour the ice cider mixture over them. Ensure the hens are well-coated. Let them marinate for at least 30 minutes, or refrigerate for a few hours for deeper flavor.

4. Remove the hens from the refrigerator and let them come to room temperature.

5. Place the game hens in a roasting pan, breast side up.

6. Roast in the preheated oven for approximately 45-55 minutes or until the internal temperature reaches 165°F (74°C).

7. Baste the hens with the marinade every 20 minutes for a glossy finish.

8. During the last 10 minutes of roasting, increase the oven temperature to 425°F (220°C) to achieve a golden skin.

9. Once done, let the hens rest for 10 minutes before carving.

10. Garnish with fresh herbs and serve the Roast Game Hen with Ice Cider Marinade—a culinary masterpiece that pays homage to the elegance of Renaissance dining.

Contemporary Ice Cider Recipes inspired by the Renaissance Culinary Traditions
3. Saffron Rice Pudding with Ice Cider Soaked Raisins

Rice pudding has been a cherished dish throughout history, gracing tables in various forms. In Renaissance times, saffron was a prized spice used to add both color and flavor to dishes. Our adaptation takes inspiration from this era, combining saffron and ice cider-soaked raisins for a dessert fit for royalty.

Ingredients:
- 1 cup Arborio rice
- 4 cups whole milk
- 1 cup heavy cream
- 1 cup sugar
- 1/2 teaspoon saffron threads
- 1/2 cup high-end ice cider
- 1/2 cup raisins

Instructions:

1. In a small bowl, steep saffron threads in a tablespoon of hot water for 10 minutes.

2. In a saucepan, combine Arborio rice, whole milk, and heavy cream. Bring to a gentle simmer over medium heat, stirring frequently.

3. Once the rice is cooked and the mixture thickens (about 20-25 minutes), add sugar and the saffron infusion. Continue cooking until the pudding reaches your desired consistency.

4. While the rice pudding is cooking, place raisins in a small bowl and pour high-end ice cider over them. Let them soak for at least 30 minutes, allowing the raisins to plump and absorb the ice cider flavor.

5. Once the rice pudding is done, fold in the ice cider-soaked raisins.

6. Remove the saffron rice pudding from heat and let it cool slightly.

7. Serve the Saffron Rice Pudding with Ice Cider-Soaked Raisins in individual bowls.

8. Optionally, garnish with a sprinkle of additional saffron threads for a touch of elegance.

9. Enjoy this golden delight—a dessert that captures the essence of Renaissance sophistication with the contemporary twist of ice cider-soaked raisins.

Contemporary Ice Cider Recipes inspired by the Renaissance Culinary Traditions
4. Renaissance Chicken and Leek Pie with Ice Cider Gravy

Chicken pies were a staple of Renaissance banquets, reflecting the era's love for hearty and flavorful dishes. Our adaptation introduces the sophistication of leeks and an indulgent ice cider gravy, elevating this classic to a level of culinary refinement reminiscent of Renaissance nobility.

Ingredients:

For the Chicken and Leek Filling:
- 2 lbs chicken, cooked and shredded
- 2 leeks, thinly sliced
- 2 tablespoons butter
- 2 tablespoons all-purpose flour
- 1 cup chicken broth
- 1/2 cup high-end ice cider
- Salt and pepper to taste
- Fresh thyme leaves for flavor

For the Pie Crust:
- 2 sheets of puff pastry

Instructions:

1. Preheat your oven to 400°F (200°C).

2. In a large skillet, melt butter over medium heat. Add sliced leeks and sauté until softened.

3. Sprinkle flour over the leeks and stir to create a roux.

4. Gradually add chicken broth and high-end ice cider, stirring continuously to avoid lumps.

5. Continue cooking until the mixture thickens into a gravy consistency.

6. Season the gravy with salt, pepper, and fresh thyme leaves.

7. Add shredded chicken to the skillet, coating it evenly in the gravy. Allow it to simmer for a few minutes.

8. Roll out one sheet of puff pastry and line a pie dish with it.

9. Pour the chicken and leek filling into the pastry-lined dish.

10. Roll out the second sheet of puff pastry and place it over the filling, sealing the edges.

11. Make a few slits on the top pastry to allow steam to escape.

12. Bake in the preheated oven for 25-30 minutes or until the pastry is golden brown and flaky.

13. Remove from the oven and let it cool slightly before serving.

14. Slice into this Renaissance Chicken and Leek Pie with Ice Cider Gravy—a culinary masterpiece that captures the essence of historical feasts with a touch of modern flair.

Contemporary Ice Cider Recipes inspired by the Renaissance Culinary Traditions
5. Barley and Ice Cider Ale

In Renaissance times, ale was a staple beverage enjoyed by people of all walks of life. Our adaptation introduces the use of barley, a common grain of the era, and the contemporary touch of high-end ice cider, adding a layer of sophistication to this classic brew.

Ingredients:
- 1 lb barley
- 1/2 lb malted barley (optional for added richness)
- 1 oz hops
- 1 gallon water
- 1 cup high-end ice cider
- 1 cup honey
- Ale yeast

Instructions:

1. In a large pot, bring water to a boil.

2. Add barley and malted barley (if using) to the boiling water. Let it simmer for 30 minutes, stirring occasionally.

3. Strain the barley from the liquid, creating a barley-infused broth.

4. Return the broth to the pot and bring it back to a simmer.

5. Add hops to the simmering broth and continue to simmer for another 30 minutes.

6. Remove the pot from heat and let it cool to room temperature.

7. Once cooled, transfer the barley and hops broth to a fermentation vessel.

8. Add high-end ice cider, honey, and ale yeast to the vessel. Mix well.

9. Seal the fermentation vessel and let the ale ferment for 1-2 weeks.

10. After fermentation, transfer the ale to bottles or a keg for carbonation.

11. Allow the Barley and Ice Cider Ale to carbonate for an additional 2 weeks.

12. Once carbonated, chill the ale and serve in mugs or glasses.

13. Savor the essence of the Renaissance with each sip of this Barley and Ice Cider Ale—a brew that brings together the simplicity of historic ales and the sophistication of modern flavors.

Contemporary Ice Cider Recipes inspired by the Renaissance Culinary Traditions

6. Honeyed Carrots with Ice Cider Glaze

Carrots were a common vegetable in Renaissance kitchens, appreciated for their sweetness. Our adaptation takes inspiration from the Renaissance love of honey-glazed vegetables, introducing the contemporary twist of an ice cider reduction for added depth and sophistication.

Ingredients:

- 1 lb carrots, peeled and sliced into rounds or sticks
- 1/2 cup high-end ice cider
- 1/4 cup honey
- 2 tablespoons butter
- Salt and pepper to taste
- Fresh parsley for garnish (optional)

Instructions:

1. In a saucepan, bring a pot of salted water to a boil.

2. Add the sliced carrots to the boiling water and cook until they are tender-crisp, about 5-7 minutes.

3. Drain the carrots and set them aside.

4. In a large skillet, melt butter over medium heat.

5. Add high-end ice cider and honey to the skillet, stirring to combine.

6. Add the cooked carrots to the skillet, tossing them in the ice cider and honey glaze.

7. Allow the carrots to simmer in the glaze for 3-5 minutes, or until they are well-coated and the glaze thickens.

8. Season with salt and pepper to taste.

9. Garnish with fresh parsley if desired.

10. Serve these Honeyed Carrots with Ice Cider Glaze—a side dish that brings the Renaissance spirit to your table with a touch of modern indulgence.

Contemporary Ice Cider Recipes inspired by the Renaissance Culinary Traditions
7. Roasted Quail with Ice Cider Fig Compote

Quail was a prized game bird enjoyed by nobility during the Renaissance, often featured in grand feasts. Our adaptation incorporates the flavors of a traditional compote, a favorite Renaissance accompaniment, enhanced by the contemporary touch of ice cider-soaked figs.

Ingredients:

For the Roasted Quail:
- 4 quails, cleaned and patted dry
- Salt and pepper to taste
- 2 tablespoons olive oil
- 1 tablespoon fresh rosemary, chopped
- 1 tablespoon fresh thyme leaves

For the Ice Cider Fig Compote:
- 1 cup dried figs, sliced
- 1/2 cup high-end ice cider
- 2 tablespoons honey
- 1/2 teaspoon cinnamon

Instructions:

1. Preheat your oven to 425°F (220°C).

2. Season the quails with salt and pepper, inside and out.

3. In a small bowl, mix olive oil, chopped rosemary, and thyme.

4. Rub the quails with the herb-infused olive oil.

5. Place the quails on a roasting pan and roast in the preheated oven for 20-25 minutes or until golden brown and cooked through.

6. While the quails are roasting, prepare the Ice Cider Fig Compote.

7. In a saucepan, combine dried figs, high-end ice cider, honey, and cinnamon.

8. Simmer the compote over medium heat until the figs are tender and the mixture has thickened into a compote consistency.

9. Once the quails are done, serve them with a generous spoonful of the Ice Cider Fig Compote.

10. Garnish with additional fresh herbs if desired.

11. Indulge in this Roasted Quail with Ice Cider Fig Compote—a dish that transports you to the grandeur of Renaissance feasts with a modern touch of sophistication.

Contemporary Ice Cider Recipes inspired by the Renaissance Culinary Traditions

8. Renaissance-Inspired Ice Cider Tiramisu

Tiramisu, with its origins in Italy, is a dessert beloved for its layers of coffee-soaked ladyfingers and mascarpone cream. Our adaptation introduces the Renaissance spirit by infusing the ladyfingers with a high-end ice cider twist, adding a layer of sweetness and complexity to this timeless treat.

Ingredients:

- 1 cup strong espresso, cooled
- 1/2 cup high-end ice cider
- 3 tablespoons sugar
- 3 large egg yolks
- 1 cup mascarpone cheese, softened
- 1 cup heavy cream
- 1 teaspoon vanilla extract
- Ladyfinger cookies
- Cocoa powder for dusting

Instructions:

1. In a bowl, combine strong espresso, high-end ice cider, and 1 tablespoon of sugar. Mix well and set aside.

2. In another bowl, whisk together egg yolks and the remaining sugar until pale and creamy.

3. Add mascarpone cheese to the egg yolk mixture and beat until smooth.

4. In a separate bowl, whip heavy cream until stiff peaks form.

5. Gently fold the whipped cream into the mascarpone mixture until well combined.

6. Dip each ladyfinger into the espresso and ice cider mixture, ensuring they are well-coated but not soggy.

7. Arrange a layer of soaked ladyfingers at the bottom of a serving dish.

8. Spread half of the mascarpone cream over the layer of ladyfingers.

9. Repeat the process with another layer of soaked ladyfingers and the remaining mascarpone cream.

10. Cover and refrigerate the Tiramisu for at least 4 hours or overnight to allow the flavors to meld.

11. Before serving, dust the top with cocoa powder for an elegant finish.

12. Indulge in this Renaissance-Inspired Ice Cider Tiramisu—a dessert that seamlessly blends the charm of the past with the sophistication of modern flavors.

Contemporary Ice Cider Recipes inspired by the Renaissance Culinary Traditions

9. Pork and Apple Ice Cider Stew

Stews were a staple of Renaissance kitchens, combining meats and fruits for a harmonious blend of flavors. Our adaptation introduces the contemporary touch of high-end ice cider, enhancing the stew with a layer of sweetness and complexity.

Ingredients:

- 2 lbs pork shoulder, cut into cubes
- Salt and pepper to taste
- 2 tablespoons olive oil
- 1 large onion, diced
- 2 cloves garlic, minced
- 2 cups high-end ice cider
- 2 cups chicken or vegetable broth
- 3 apples, peeled, cored, and sliced
- 1 teaspoon dried thyme
- 1 teaspoon dried rosemary
- 1 bay leaf
- Chopped fresh parsley for garnish (optional)

Instructions:

1. Season pork cubes with salt and pepper.

2. In a large pot, heat olive oil over medium-high heat. Add pork cubes and brown on all sides.

3. Add diced onion and minced garlic to the pot. Sauté until the onions are translucent.

4. Pour in high-end ice cider and broth, scraping the bottom of the pot to release any browned bits.

5. Add sliced apples, dried thyme, dried rosemary, and the bay leaf to the pot. Stir well.

6. Bring the stew to a boil, then reduce the heat to low. Cover and simmer for 1.5 to 2 hours, or until the pork is tender.

7. Check the seasoning and adjust with salt and pepper if needed.

8. Discard the bay leaf before serving.

9. Garnish with chopped fresh parsley if desired.

10. Serve this Pork and Apple Ice Cider Stew—a dish that captures the warmth and richness of Renaissance flavors, elevated by the contemporary addition of high-end ice cider.

Contemporary Ice Cider Recipes inspired by the Renaissance Culinary Traditions

10. Renaissance Apple Tart with Ice Cider Glaze

Fruit tarts were a common feature in Renaissance banquets, showcasing the bounty of the season. Our adaptation introduces the contemporary elegance of high-end ice cider, creating a glaze that encapsulates the sweet essence of historical opulence.

Ingredients:

For the Tart:
- 1 pre-made pie crust or homemade pastry dough
- 4-5 medium-sized apples, peeled, cored, and thinly sliced
- 1/4 cup sugar
- 1 teaspoon ground cinnamon (the surprise ingredient)
- 2 tablespoons butter, cut into small pieces

For the Ice Cider Glaze:
- 1/2 cup high-end ice cider
- 1/4 cup apricot preserves
- 1 tablespoon lemon juice

Instructions:

1. Preheat your oven to 375°F (190°C).

2. Roll out the pie crust and place it in a tart pan, trimming any excess.

3. In a bowl, toss the sliced apples with sugar and ground cinnamon.

4. Arrange the apple slices on the pie crust in an overlapping pattern.

5. Dot the apples with small pieces of butter.

6. Bake in the preheated oven for 25-30 minutes or until the crust is golden and the apples are tender.

7. While the tart is baking, prepare the Ice Cider Glaze.

8. In a saucepan, combine high-end ice cider, apricot preserves, and lemon juice. Simmer over medium heat until the mixture thickens into a glaze.

9. Once the tart is done baking, remove it from the oven and let it cool slightly.

10. Brush the warm tart with the Ice Cider Glaze, ensuring an even coating.

11. Allow the tart to cool completely before serving.

12. Slice into this Renaissance Apple Tart with Ice Cider Glaze—a dessert that combines the simplicity of the past with the surprise of contemporary flavors, creating a sweet surprise for your taste buds.

Contemporary Ice Cider Recipes inspired by the Victorian Culinary Traditions

Step into the grandeur of the Victorian era as we reimagine classic dishes with a modern twist— the addition of exquisite ice cider. Known for their elaborate feasts and intricate recipes, the Victorians embraced the art of culinary craftsmanship. In this collection, we present 10 savory and 10 sweet recipes that pay homage to the opulence of the time, enhanced by the nuanced flavors of high-end ice cider.

Savory Selections:

1. Ice Cider-Infused Beef Wellington with Mushroom Duxelles:
Tender beef fillet, marinated in a reduction of ice cider, coated with a layer of mushroom duxelles, wrapped in puff pastry, and baked.

2. Chicken Pot Pie with Flaky Ice Cider Crust:
Tender chunks of chicken, vegetables, and a creamy sauce infused with ice cider encased in a flaky pastry crust, baked until golden brown.

3. Deviled Eggs with Mustard, Cress, and Ice Cider Drizzle:
Hard-boiled eggs halved and filled with a mixture of yolks, mustard, mayonnaise, and topped with fresh cress, drizzled with a reduction of ice cider.

4. Shepherd's Pie with Mashed Ice Cider Potatoes:
Ground meat, vegetables, and gravy topped with creamy mashed potatoes infused with a hint of ice cider, then baked until golden.

5. Victorian Lobster Newberg with Ice Cider Cream Sauce:
Lobster pieces cooked in a rich, brandy-infused cream sauce with egg yolks, served over buttered toast, featuring a touch of ice cider sweetness.

6. Welsh Rarebit with Ale and Ice Cider Reduction:
Toasted bread smothered in a savory sauce made from melted cheese, ale, mustard, and spices, finished with a drizzle of ice cider reduction.

7. Savoury Ice Cider Aspic with Game Meats:
A clear jelly made from broth, set with game meats, vegetables, and herbs, enhanced with the subtle sweetness of ice cider.

8. Kedgeree with Smoked Fish and Ice Cider Curry Spices:
A rice dish with flaked smoked fish, hard-boiled eggs, and curry spices, reflecting Victorian fascination with Indian cuisine, with a touch of ice cider.

9. Oysters Rockefeller with Ice Cider Infusion:
Oysters topped with a mixture of herbs, breadcrumbs, and butter, then baked until bubbly, featuring a hint of ice cider complexity.

10. Ice Cider-Glazed Cornish Pasty:
A pastry filled with meat, potatoes, and vegetables, traditionally crimped along the edge, finished with a glaze made from reduced ice cider.

Sweet Delights:

1. Victoria Sponge Cake with Ice Cider-Infused Whipped Cream:
A classic sponge cake filled with strawberry jam and whipped cream infused with a touch of ice cider.

2. Eccles Cakes with Ice Cider-Soaked Currants:
Flaky pastry filled with a mixture of currants soaked in ice cider, sugar, and spices.

3. Trifle with Sherry-Soaked Sponge and Ice Cider-Infused Custard:
Layers of sherry-soaked sponge cake, custard infused with ice cider, fruit, and whipped cream.

4. Bakewell Tart with Almond Paste and Ice Cider Drizzle:
A tart filled with almond paste, raspberry jam, and topped with a layer of icing, drizzled with a reduction of ice cider.

5. Gingerbread Men with Ice Cider Icing:
Spiced cookies shaped like men and decorated with icing infused with the fruity notes of ice cider.

6. Queen of Puddings with Ice Cider Custard:
A dessert featuring a layer of breadcrumbs, custard infused with ice cider, and a topping of meringue.

7. Battenberg Cake with Ice Cider Marzipan:
A checkered cake made of pink and yellow sponge wrapped in marzipan infused with the subtle sweetness of ice cider.

8. Raspberry Fool with Ice Cider Whipped Cream:
Whipped cream folded with raspberry puree, creating a light and fruity dessert, accentuated by the addition of ice cider.

9. Custard Tart with Ice Cider Nutmeg:
A pastry crust filled with creamy custard, often dusted with nutmeg and subtly sweetened with a touch of ice cider.

10. Meringue Nests with Berries and Ice Cider Syrup:
Crispy meringue nests filled with fresh berries and a dollop of whipped cream, drizzled with a syrup made from reduced ice cider.

Embark on a culinary journey, where tradition meets innovation, and the allure of Victorian gastronomy is heightened by the essence of ice cider. These recipes promise a feast that transcends time, inviting you to savor the flavors of a bygone era made exquisite by the inclusion of this refined and luxurious ingredient.

Contemporary Ice Cider Recipes inspired by the Savory Victorian Culinary Traditions

1. Ice Cider-Infused Beef Wellington with Mushroom Duxelles

Beef Wellington, a dish often associated with grand Victorian banquets, was a testament to culinary indulgence. Our contemporary adaptation introduces the luxurious touch of ice cider, bringing a subtle sweetness that complements the savory profile of the original.

Ingredients:

- 2 lbs beef fillet
- Salt and pepper to taste
- 1 cup high-end ice cider
- 2 tablespoons olive oil
- 1 pound mushrooms, finely chopped
- 4 cloves garlic, minced
- 1 package puff pastry sheets, thawed
- 1 egg, beaten (for egg wash)

Instructions:

1. Season the beef fillet with salt and pepper. Sear it on all sides in a hot pan with olive oil until browned. Let it cool.

2. In the same pan, sauté mushrooms and garlic until all moisture evaporates. Add ice cider and cook until it forms a thick consistency. Let it cool.

3. Roll out the puff pastry and spread the mushroom mixture on it. Place the seared beef in the center.

4. Wrap the beef in the pastry, sealing the edges. Brush with beaten egg for a golden finish.

5. Bake in a preheated oven at 400°F (200°C) for 25-30 minutes or until the pastry is golden and the beef is cooked to your liking.

6. Let it rest for a few minutes before slicing.

7. Serve this contemporary Ice Cider-Infused Beef Wellington, a delightful fusion of Victorian decadence and modern culinary innovation.

Contemporary Ice Cider Recipes inspired by the Savory Victorian Culinary Traditions

2. Chicken Pot Pie with Flaky Ice Cider Crust

Chicken Pot Pie, a staple in Victorian households, epitomized the era's emphasis on hearty, flavorful dishes. Our contemporary rendition adds a layer of refinement with the inclusion of ice cider, elevating this beloved classic to new heights.

Ingredients:

- 2 cups cooked chicken, shredded
- 1 cup carrots, diced
- 1 cup peas
- 1/2 cup butter
- 1/2 cup all-purpose flour
- 1/2 teaspoon salt
- 1/4 teaspoon black pepper
- 1/4 teaspoon celery seed
- 1/4 teaspoon onion powder
- 1/4 teaspoon garlic powder
- 1 3/4 cups chicken broth
- 2/3 cup high-end ice cider
- 2/3 cup milk

For the Crust:
- 2 1/2 cups all-purpose flour
- 1/2 teaspoon salt
- 1 cup cold butter, cubed
- 1/2 cup ice water
- 2 tablespoons high-end ice cider

Instructions:

1. In a large saucepan, melt butter over medium heat. Stir in flour, salt, pepper, celery seed, onion powder, and garlic powder until well combined.

2. Gradually whisk in chicken broth, ice cider, and milk. Simmer until the mixture thickens.

3. Add chicken, carrots, and peas. Simmer until vegetables are tender. Remove from heat and let it cool.

4. For the crust, combine flour and salt. Cut in the butter until the mixture resembles coarse crumbs.

5. Gradually add ice water and ice cider, tossing with a fork until a ball forms. Divide the dough in half.

6. Roll out one half to line a pie dish. Pour in the cooled chicken mixture.

7. Roll out the remaining dough for the top crust. Place it over the filling and seal the edges. Cut slits in the top for ventilation.

8. Bake in a preheated oven at 425°F (220°C) for 30-35 minutes or until the crust is golden brown.

9. Allow it to cool for a few minutes before serving.

Delight in the modern comfort of Chicken Pot Pie with Flaky Ice Cider Crust—a timeless dish that seamlessly blends Victorian heartiness with the contemporary touch of high-end ice cider.

Contemporary Ice Cider Recipes inspired by the Savory Victorian Culinary Traditions

3. Deviled Eggs with Mustard, Cress, and Ice Cider Drizzle

Deviled Eggs, a beloved Victorian *hors d'oeuvre*, showcased the era's penchant for intricate flavors. Our modern interpretation introduces a hint of sweetness with an ice cider drizzle, elevating this timeless dish to new heights of culinary delight.

Ingredients:

- 6 hard-boiled eggs, peeled and halved
- 2 tablespoons mayonnaise
- 1 teaspoon Dijon mustard
- Salt and pepper to taste
- Fresh cress for garnish
- High-end ice cider for drizzling

Instructions:

1. Cut the hard-boiled eggs in half lengthwise. Remove the yolks and place them in a bowl.

2. Mash the yolks and mix in mayonnaise, Dijon mustard, salt, and pepper until smooth.

3. Spoon the yolk mixture back into the egg whites or use a piping bag for a neater presentation.

4. Garnish each deviled egg with fresh cress.

5. Just before serving, delicately drizzle a small amount of high-end ice cider over the top of each deviled egg.

6. Arrange on a platter and serve immediately.

Indulge in the exquisite flavors of Deviled Eggs with Mustard, Cress, and Ice Cider Drizzle—a contemporary delight that marries Victorian charm with the luxurious touch of high-end ice cider.

Contemporary Ice Cider Recipes inspired by the Savory Victorian Culinary Traditions

4. Shepherd's Pie with Mashed Ice Cider Potatoes

Shepherd's Pie, a staple in Victorian households, was a comforting dish that reflected the era's emphasis on hearty, flavorful meals. Our contemporary rendition elevates this beloved classic with the addition of mashed potatoes featuring the nuanced sweetness of ice cider.

Ingredients:

- 1 lb ground meat (lamb traditionally, or beef)
- 1 onion, finely chopped
- 2 carrots, diced
- 1 cup peas
- 2 cloves garlic, minced
- 2 tablespoons tomato paste
- 1 cup beef or vegetable broth
- 1 tablespoon Worcestershire sauce
- Salt and pepper to taste
- Fresh thyme leaves for garnish

For the Mashed Potatoes:
- 4 large potatoes, peeled and chopped
- 1/2 cup butter
- 1/2 cup milk
- Salt and pepper to taste
- 1/4 cup high-end ice cider

Instructions:

1. Preheat the oven to 400°F (200°C).

2. In a large skillet, brown the ground meat over medium heat. Add onions, carrots, peas, and garlic. Cook until vegetables are tender.

3. Stir in tomato paste, beef or vegetable broth, Worcestershire sauce, salt, and pepper. Simmer until the mixture thickens.

4. Meanwhile, boil the potatoes until tender. Mash with butter, milk, salt, and pepper. Gradually add high-end ice cider until smooth.

5. Transfer the meat mixture to a baking dish. Spread the mashed potatoes over the top, creating a smooth layer.

6. Bake for 20-25 minutes or until the mashed potatoes are golden brown.

7. Garnish with fresh thyme leaves before serving.

Delight in the comfort of Shepherd's Pie with Mashed Ice Cider Potatoes—a modern reinterpretation that seamlessly blends Victorian warmth with the contemporary sophistication of high-end ice cider.

Contemporary Ice Cider Recipes inspired by the Savory Victorian Culinary Traditions
5. Victorian Lobster Newberg with Ice Cider Cream Sauce

Lobster Newberg, a culinary sensation in Victorian times, epitomized the era's penchant for lavish dining experiences. Our modern adaptation pays homage to this classic by introducing the exquisite touch of high-end ice cider to elevate the cream sauce, creating a dish that seamlessly bridges the gap between eras.

Ingredients:

- 2 lobster tails, meat removed and chopped
- 2 tablespoons butter
- 2 tablespoons brandy
- 1 cup heavy cream
- 1/4 cup high-end ice cider
- 2 egg yolks
- Salt and white pepper to taste
- Chopped chives for garnish
- Toasted bread or puff pastry for serving

Instructions:

1. In a skillet, melt butter over medium heat. Add lobster pieces and cook until opaque.

2. Pour in brandy and flambé the lobster. Allow the flames to subside.

3. In a separate bowl, whisk together egg yolks, heavy cream, and high-end ice cider.

4. Slowly pour the cream mixture into the skillet, stirring continuously until the sauce thickens.

5. Season with salt and white pepper to taste.

6. Serve the Lobster Newberg over toasted bread or puff pastry.

7. Garnish with chopped chives before serving.

Indulge in the lavish experience of Victorian Lobster Newberg with Ice Cider Cream Sauce—a contemporary re-imagining that brings the decadence of the past into the present, enriched by the nuanced sweetness of high-end ice cider.

Contemporary Ice Cider Recipes inspired by the Savory Victorian Culinary Traditions

6. Welsh Rarebit with Ale and Ice Cider Reduction

Welsh Rarebit, a staple in Welsh cuisine, showcased the simplicity and richness of the region's culinary offerings. Our contemporary twist introduces complexity by combining ale and high-end ice cider reduction, adding layers of flavor to this timeless dish.

Ingredients:

- 2 tablespoons butter
- 2 tablespoons all-purpose flour
- 1 teaspoon mustard powder
- 1/2 teaspoon cayenne pepper
- 1/2 cup ale
- 1/4 cup high-end ice cider
- 2 cups sharp cheddar cheese, grated
- 4 slices of your favorite bread, toasted

Instructions:

1. In a saucepan over medium heat, melt butter. Stir in flour, mustard powder, and cayenne pepper until smooth.

2. Gradually whisk in ale and high-end ice cider, stirring constantly until the mixture thickens.

3. Reduce heat to low and gradually add grated cheddar cheese. Stir until the cheese is melted and the sauce is smooth.

4. Remove from heat and let the rarebit mixture sit for a few minutes.

5. Toast the bread slices to your liking.
6. Pour the rarebit mixture over the toasted bread slices.

7. Optionally, place the Welsh Rarebit under the broiler for a minute or two until bubbly and lightly browned.

8. Serve immediately and savor the contemporary twist of Welsh Rarebit with Ale and Ice Cider Reduction.

Delight in the culinary fusion of tradition and innovation with the nuanced sweetness of high-end ice cider in this modern Welsh Rarebit adaptation.

Contemporary Ice Cider Recipes inspired by the Savory Victorian Culinary Traditions

7. Savoury Ice Cider Aspic with Game Meats

Aspics were a hallmark of Victorian culinary extravagance, showcasing intricate presentations and a delicate balance of flavors. Our modern interpretation introduces a touch of luxury with the inclusion of high-end ice cider, enhancing the depth of this classic dish.

Ingredients:

- 4 cups rich game broth (venison, pheasant, or a combination)
- 1/2 cup high-end ice cider
- 2 envelopes unflavored gelatin
- 1 cup mixed cooked game meats (venison, duck, rabbit), diced
- Fresh herbs (thyme, rosemary) for garnish
- Salt and pepper to taste

Instructions:

1. In a saucepan, heat the game broth until simmering. Remove from heat and add high-end ice cider.

2. Sprinkle the gelatin evenly over the broth and let it sit for a minute to bloom.

3. Stir the mixture over low heat until the gelatin is completely dissolved.

4. Season with salt and pepper to taste.

5. Let the broth cool to room temperature.

6. Divide the diced game meats among serving molds or a large serving dish.

7. Pour the cooled broth over the game meats.

8. Refrigerate until fully set, at least 4 hours or overnight.

9. Before serving, dip the molds in warm water for a few seconds to loosen the aspic.

10. Invert the aspic onto a serving plate or unmold onto individual plates.

11. Garnish with fresh herbs.

Delight in the refined sophistication of Savory Ice Cider Aspic with Game Meats—a contemporary interpretation that pays homage to Victorian culinary artistry.

Contemporary Ice Cider Recipes inspired by the Savory Victorian Culinary Traditions
8. Kedgeree with Smoked Fish and Ice Cider Curry Spices

Kedgeree, inspired by Indian cuisine, became a beloved dish in Victorian England, combining the exotic allure of spices with the comfort of home-cooked meals. Our contemporary adaptation elevates this classic with the addition of ice cider, creating a unique flavor profile that resonates with modern palates.

Ingredients:

- 1 cup basmati rice
- 1 1/2 cups water
- 1/2 cup high-end ice cider
- 1 tablespoon vegetable oil
- 1 onion, finely chopped
- 2 teaspoons curry powder
- 1/2 teaspoon turmeric
- 1/2 teaspoon cumin
- 1/2 teaspoon coriander
- 1/2 teaspoon smoked paprika
- 1 cup smoked fish (haddock or salmon), flaked
- 4 hard-boiled eggs, chopped
- Fresh parsley for garnish
- Salt and pepper to taste

Instructions:

1. Rinse the basmati rice under cold water until the water runs clear.

2. In a saucepan, combine the rice, water, and high-end ice cider. Bring to a boil, then reduce heat to low, cover, and simmer until the rice is cooked and the liquid is absorbed.

3. In a large skillet, heat vegetable oil over medium heat. Add chopped onion and sauté until softened.

4. Add curry powder, turmeric, cumin, coriander, and smoked paprika to the skillet. Stir to coat the onions in the spices.

5. Add the flaked smoked fish to the skillet and cook briefly until heated through.

6. Gently fold the cooked rice and chopped hard-boiled eggs into the skillet, mixing until well combined.

7. Season with salt and pepper to taste.

8. Garnish with fresh parsley before serving.

Contemporary Ice Cider Recipes inspired by the Savory Victorian Culinary Traditions

9. Oysters Rockefeller with Ice Cider Infusion

Oysters Rockefeller, born in the Gilded Age, epitomized the luxurious dining experiences of the Victorian era. Our contemporary adaptation introduces the subtle sweetness of high-end ice cider, adding a layer of sophistication to this timeless delicacy.

Ingredients:

- 12 fresh oysters, shucked
- 1/2 cup fresh spinach, chopped
- 1/4 cup fresh parsley, chopped
- 1/4 cup green onions, chopped
- 1/4 cup breadcrumbs
- 2 tablespoons butter, melted
- 1/4 cup high-end ice cider
- 1/4 cup grated Parmesan cheese
- Salt and pepper to taste
- Crushed ice for serving

Instructions:

1. Preheat the oven to 450°F (232°C).

2. In a bowl, combine chopped spinach, parsley, green onions, breadcrumbs, melted butter, and high-end ice cider. Mix well.

3. Place shucked oysters on a baking sheet lined with rock salt or crumpled foil to stabilize them.

4. Spoon the spinach and breadcrumb mixture over each oyster, covering them evenly.

5. Sprinkle grated Parmesan cheese over the top of each oyster.

6. Bake in the preheated oven for 10-12 minutes or until the topping is golden brown and the oysters are cooked.

7. Remove from the oven and let them cool slightly.

8. Serve on a bed of crushed ice for a sophisticated presentation.

Indulge in the elevated indulgence of Oysters Rockefeller with Ice Cider Infusion—a contemporary interpretation that pays homage to the opulence of Victorian dining, enhanced by the nuanced sweetness of high-end ice cider.

Contemporary Ice Cider Recipes inspired by the Savory Victorian Culinary Traditions

10. Ice Cider-Glazed Cornish Pasty

Cornish Pasties, born out of the mining communities in Cornwall, were cherished for their hearty simplicity. Our contemporary adaptation pays homage to this enduring dish, infusing it with a subtle sweetness from high-end ice cider, adding a layer of complexity to the familiar flavors.

Ingredients:

- 1 pound beef or lamb, diced
- 1 onion, finely chopped
- 2 potatoes, peeled and diced
- 1 carrot, peeled and diced
- 1 tablespoon all-purpose flour
- Salt and pepper to taste
- 2 sheets of ready-made puff pastry
- 1/2 cup high-end ice cider
- 1 egg, beaten (for egg wash)

Instructions:

1. Preheat the oven to 400°F (200°C).

2. In a bowl, combine diced meat, chopped onion, diced potatoes, diced carrot, flour, salt, and pepper.

3. Roll out the puff pastry sheets on a floured surface.

4. Cut out rounds from the pastry sheets to form the pasty bases.

5. Spoon the meat and vegetable mixture onto one half of each pastry round.

6. Brush the edges of the pastry with beaten egg, then fold the other half over the filling, creating a semi-circle. Press the edges to seal.

7. Place the pasties on a baking sheet lined with parchment paper.

8. Bake in the preheated oven for 25-30 minutes or until the pastry is golden brown.

9. While the pasties are baking, simmer high-end ice cider in a saucepan until it reduces to a glaze consistency.

10. Once the pasties are out of the oven, brush them with the ice cider glaze for a glossy finish.

11. Allow the pasties to cool slightly before serving.

Savor the harmonious fusion of flavors in the Ice Cider-Glazed Cornish Pasty—a contemporary twist that honors the past while embracing the sophistication of high-end ice cider.

Contemporary Ice Cider Recipes inspired by the Sweet Victorian Culinary Traditions
1. Victoria Sponge Cake with Ice Cider-Infused Whipped Cream

The Victoria Sponge Cake, named after Queen Victoria, was a symbol of Victorian refinement and simplicity. Our contemporary adaptation pays homage to this timeless dessert by introducing a subtle infusion of high-end ice cider, elevating it to a dessert fit for royalty.

Ingredients:

For the Sponge Cake:
- 1 cup unsalted butter, softened
- 1 cup granulated sugar
- 4 large eggs
- 2 cups all-purpose flour
- 2 teaspoons baking powder
- 1/2 teaspoon salt
- 1/2 cup whole milk
- 1 teaspoon vanilla extract

For the Whipped Cream:
- 2 cups heavy whipping cream
- 1/4 cup high-end ice cider
- 1/4 cup powdered sugar

Instructions:

For the Sponge Cake:
1. Preheat the oven to 350°F (180°C). Grease and flour two 9-inch round cake pans.

2. In a large bowl, cream together the softened butter and granulated sugar until light and fluffy.

3. Add the eggs one at a time, beating well after each addition.

4. In a separate bowl, whisk together the flour, baking powder, and salt.

5. Gradually add the dry ingredients to the wet ingredients, alternating with the milk. Begin and end with the dry ingredients. Mix in the vanilla extract.

6. Divide the batter evenly between the prepared cake pans and smooth the tops.

7. Bake in the preheated oven for 25-30 minutes or until a toothpick inserted into the center comes out clean.

8. Allow the cakes to cool in the pans for 10 minutes before transferring them to a wire rack to cool completely.

For the Whipped Cream:
1. In a chilled bowl, whip the heavy whipping cream until soft peaks form.

2. Gently fold in the high-end ice cider and powdered sugar until well combined.

Assembly:
1. Place one cooled sponge layer on a serving plate.

2. Spread a generous layer of ice cider-infused whipped cream over the first layer.

3. Top with the second sponge layer.

4. Dust the top with powdered sugar for a classic finish.

Indulge in the sophistication of Victoria Sponge Cake with Ice Cider-Infused Whipped Cream—a contemporary masterpiece that retains the grace of a bygone era, now elevated with the subtle sweetness of high-end ice cider.

Contemporary Ice Cider Recipes inspired by the Sweet Victorian Culinary Traditions
2. Eccles Cakes with Ice Cider-Soaked Currants

Eccles Cakes, born in the town of Eccles in Greater Manchester, have been a cherished treat since the 18th century. Our contemporary adaptation pays homage to this beloved pastry by infusing the currants with the nuanced sweetness of high-end ice cider, adding a layer of sophistication to this classic.

Ingredients:

- 2 cups dried currants
- 1/2 cup high-end ice cider
- 1 cup unsalted butter, chilled and diced
- 2 cups all-purpose flour
- 1/4 teaspoon salt
- 1 cup granulated sugar
- 1 egg, beaten (for egg wash)
- Powdered sugar for dusting

Instructions:

1. In a bowl, combine dried currants and high-end ice cider. Allow the currants to soak and absorb the ice cider for at least 1 hour or overnight.

2. Preheat the oven to 400°F (200°C).

3. In a large mixing bowl, combine the chilled and diced unsalted butter with the flour and salt. Use your fingertips to rub the butter into the flour until the mixture resembles breadcrumbs.

4. Stir in the granulated sugar.

5. Strain the soaked currants, reserving the liquid for later use.

6. Roll out the pastry on a floured surface to about 1/8 inch thickness.

7. Cut out rounds from the pastry, approximately 4 inches in diameter.

8. Place a spoonful of the ice cider-soaked currants in the center of each pastry round.

9. Fold the pastry over the currants to form a half-moon shape and press the edges to seal.

10. Place the filled pastries on a baking sheet lined with parchment paper.

11. Brush each pastry with beaten egg for a golden finish.

12. Use a sharp knife to make a couple of slits on the top of each pastry to allow steam to escape.

13. Bake in the preheated oven for 15-20 minutes or until the pastry is golden brown and crisp.

14. While the cakes are baking, heat the reserved ice cider liquid in a small saucepan until it thickens to a syrupy consistency.

15. Once out of the oven, brush each Eccles Cake with the ice cider reduction for a glossy sheen.

16. Allow the cakes to cool slightly before dusting with powdered sugar.

Savor the irresistible charm of Eccles Cakes with Ice Cider-Soaked Currants—a contemporary delight that encapsulates the timeless allure of this cherished British pastry, enriched by the subtle sweetness of high-end ice cider.

Contemporary Ice Cider Recipes inspired by the Sweet Victorian Culinary Traditions
3. Trifle with Sherry-Soaked Sponge and Ice Cider-Infused Custard

Trifle, with its roots traced back to the 16th century, has been a symbol of English dessert elegance. Our contemporary adaptation pays homage to this timeless treat by introducing the subtle infusion of high-end ice cider, adding a layer of complexity to the traditional layers of sponge and custard.

Ingredients:
For the Sherry-Soaked Sponge:
- 1 sponge cake (store-bought or homemade)
- 1/2 cup sherry

For the Ice Cider-Infused Custard:
- 2 cups whole milk
- 1 cup heavy cream
- 4 large egg yolks
- 1/2 cup granulated sugar
- 1/4 cup cornstarch
- 1/4 cup high-end ice cider
- 1 teaspoon vanilla extract

For Assembly:
- Fresh berries (strawberries, raspberries, or blueberries)
- Whipped cream for topping

Instructions:
For the Sherry-Soaked Sponge:
1. Cut the sponge cake into bite-sized cubes.

2. In a shallow dish, pour the sherry over the sponge cake cubes, ensuring they are well-soaked. Set aside.

For the Ice Cider-Infused Custard:
1. In a saucepan, heat the whole milk and heavy cream over medium heat until it just begins to simmer. Do not boil.

2. In a bowl, whisk together the egg yolks, granulated sugar, and cornstarch until smooth.

3. Slowly pour the hot milk mixture into the egg yolk mixture, whisking constantly.
4. Return the mixture to the saucepan and cook over medium heat, stirring constantly, until it thickens to a custard consistency.

5. Remove from heat and stir in the high-end ice cider and vanilla extract.

6. Allow the custard to cool to room temperature.

For Assembly:
1. In serving glasses or a trifle dish, layer the sherry-soaked sponge cake cubes.

2. Pour a portion of the ice cider-infused custard over the sponge cake layer.

3. Repeat the layers until the glasses or dish are filled.

4. Top with fresh berries and a dollop of whipped cream.

5. Chill in the refrigerator for at least 2 hours before serving.

Savor the sophistication of Trifle with Sherry-Soaked Sponge and Ice Cider-Infused Custard—a contemporary twist on a timeless favorite that harmonizes the rich history of trifle with the nuanced sweetness of high-end ice cider.

Contemporary Ice Cider Recipes inspired by the Sweet Victorian Culinary Traditions

4. Bakewell Tart with Almond Paste and Ice Cider Drizzle

The Bakewell Tart, originating from the town of Bakewell in Derbyshire, has been a cherished treat since the 19th century. Our contemporary adaptation pays homage to this timeless dessert by infusing the almond filling with the nuanced sweetness of high-end ice cider, adding a layer of complexity to the traditional combination of almond and pastry.

Ingredients:
For the Pastry:
- 1 1/2 cups all-purpose flour
- 1/2 cup unsalted butter, chilled and diced
- 1/4 cup granulated sugar
- 1 large egg, beaten

For the Almond Filling:
- 1 cup almond flour
- 1/2 cup granulated sugar
- 1/2 cup unsalted butter, softened
- 2 large eggs
- 1 teaspoon almond extract

For the Icing:
- 1 cup powdered sugar
- 2 tablespoons high-end ice cider

Instructions:
For the Pastry:
1. In a food processor, combine the all-purpose flour, chilled and diced unsalted butter, and granulated sugar. Pulse until the mixture resembles breadcrumbs.

2. Add the beaten egg and pulse until the dough comes together.

3. Turn the pastry out onto a floured surface and knead briefly to form a smooth ball.

4. Wrap the pastry in plastic wrap and refrigerate for at least 30 minutes.

For the Almond Filling:
1. Preheat the oven to 350°F (180°C). Grease a tart pan.

2. In a bowl, combine almond flour, granulated sugar, softened unsalted butter, eggs, and almond extract. Mix until well combined.

For Assembly:
1. Roll out the chilled pastry on a floured surface to fit the tart pan.

2. Press the pastry into the pan and trim any excess.

3. Spread the almond filling evenly over the pastry.

4. Bake in the preheated oven for 25-30 minutes or until the filling is set and the pastry is golden brown.

5. Allow the tart to cool completely.

For the Icing:
1. In a bowl, whisk together powdered sugar and high-end ice cider until smooth.

2. Drizzle the icing over the cooled tart.

Indulge in the luxurious bliss of Bakewell Tart with Almond Paste and Ice Cider Drizzle—a contemporary masterpiece that pays homage to the traditional charm of Bakewell, now enriched by the subtle sweetness of high-end ice cider.

Contemporary Ice Cider Recipes inspired by the Sweet Victorian Culinary Traditions
5. Gingerbread Men with Ice Cider Icing

Gingerbread Men have been a festive favorite since medieval times, often associated with holidays and celebrations. Our contemporary adaptation pays homage to this timeless tradition by introducing an ice cider icing that elevates the flavor profile, creating a delightful synergy of warmth and sophistication.

Ingredients:

For the Gingerbread Dough:
- 3 cups all-purpose flour
- 1 teaspoon baking powder
- 1/2 teaspoon baking soda
- 1/4 teaspoon salt
- 1 tablespoon ground ginger
- 1 1/2 teaspoons ground cinnamon
- 1/2 teaspoon ground cloves
- 1/2 cup unsalted butter, softened
- 1/2 cup brown sugar, packed
- 1 large egg
- 1/2 cup molasses

For the Ice Cider Icing:
- 1 cup powdered sugar
- 2 tablespoons high-end ice cider

Instructions:

For the Gingerbread Dough:
1. In a bowl, whisk together the flour, baking powder, baking soda, salt, ground ginger, ground cinnamon, and ground cloves.

2. In another bowl, beat the softened unsalted butter and brown sugar until light and fluffy.

3. Add the egg and molasses to the butter-sugar mixture, mixing until well combined.

4. Gradually add the dry ingredients to the wet ingredients, mixing until a dough forms.

5. Divide the dough into two portions, wrap in plastic wrap, and refrigerate for at least 1 hour.

For Baking:
1. Preheat the oven to 350°F (180°C) and line baking sheets with parchment paper.

2. Roll out one portion of the chilled dough on a floured surface to about 1/4 inch thickness.

3. Use gingerbread men cookie cutters to cut out shapes and place them on the prepared baking sheets.

4. Bake for 8-10 minutes or until the edges are golden brown.

5. Allow the cookies to cool completely.

For the Ice Cider Icing:
1. In a bowl, whisk together powdered sugar and high-end ice cider until smooth.

2. Transfer the icing to a piping bag and decorate the cooled gingerbread men as desired.

Embrace the festive joy with Gingerbread Men with Ice Cider Icing—a delightful blend of tradition and innovation that captures the essence of the season, enriched by the subtle sweetness of high-end ice cider.

Contemporary Ice Cider Recipes inspired by the Sweet Victorian Culinary Traditions

6. Queen of Puddings with Ice Cider Custard

The Queen of Puddings, with its roots traced back to the 19th century, has been a symbol of British dessert elegance. Our contemporary adaptation pays homage to this timeless treat by infusing the custard with the nuanced sweetness of high-end ice cider, adding a layer of complexity to the traditional combination of custard, breadcrumbs, and jam.

Ingredients:

For the Custard:
- 2 cups whole milk
- 1/2 cup granulated sugar
- 4 large egg yolks
- 2 tablespoons cornstarch
- 1/4 cup high-end ice cider
- 1 teaspoon vanilla extract

For the Breadcrumb Layer:
- 2 cups fresh breadcrumbs
- 1/2 cup unsalted butter, melted
- Zest of one lemon

For the Jam Layer:
- 1 cup fruit jam (raspberry or red currant work well)

Instructions:

For the Custard:
1. In a saucepan, heat the whole milk until it just begins to simmer. Do not boil.

2. In a bowl, whisk together granulated sugar, egg yolks, and cornstarch until smooth.

3. Slowly pour the hot milk into the egg yolk mixture, whisking constantly.

4. Return the mixture to the saucepan and cook over medium heat, stirring constantly, until it thickens to a custard consistency.

5. Remove from heat and stir in the high-end ice cider and vanilla extract.

6. Allow the custard to cool to room temperature.

For the Breadcrumb Layer:
1. In a bowl, combine fresh breadcrumbs, melted unsalted butter, and lemon zest.

2. Spread the breadcrumb mixture evenly in a baking dish.

For Assembly:
1. Preheat the oven to 350°F (180°C).

2. Bake the breadcrumb layer for 15-20 minutes or until golden brown.

3. Remove from the oven and let it cool slightly.

4. Spread the fruit jam over the breadcrumb layer.

5. Pour the cooled ice cider custard over the jam layer.

6. Return the dish to the oven and bake for an additional 20-25 minutes or until the custard is set.

7. Allow the Queen of Puddings to cool before serving.

Indulge in the regal decadence of Queen of Puddings with Ice Cider Custard—a contemporary masterpiece that pays homage to the classic elegance of this cherished British dessert, now enriched by the subtle sweetness of high-end ice cider.

Contemporary Ice Cider Recipes inspired by the Sweet Victorian Culinary Traditions

7. Battenberg Cake with Ice Cider Marzipan

The Battenberg Cake, originating in Victorian England, has been a symbol of elegance and precision. Our contemporary adaptation pays homage to this iconic cake by introducing marzipan infused with the nuanced sweetness of high-end ice cider, elevating the flavor profile and creating a delightful symphony of almond and fruit notes.

Ingredients:
For the Almond Sponge Cake:

- 1 cup unsalted butter, softened
- 1 cup granulated sugar
- 3 large eggs
- 1 1/2 cups self-rising flour
- 1 cup ground almonds
- 1 teaspoon almond extract
- Red food coloring

For the Ice Cider Marzipan:
- 2 cups almond paste
- 1 cup powdered sugar
- 2 tablespoons high-end ice cider
- Yellow food coloring

For Assembly:
- Apricot jam for spreading

Instructions:
For the Almond Sponge Cake:

1. Preheat the oven to 350°F (180°C). Grease and line a square baking pan.

2. In a bowl, cream together softened unsalted butter and granulated sugar until light and fluffy.

3. Add the eggs one at a time, beating well after each addition.

4. Fold in self-rising flour, ground almonds, and almond extract until well combined.

5. Divide the batter in half. Tint one half with red food coloring until you achieve the desired color.

6. Spoon each colored batter into half of the prepared baking pan.

7. Bake for 25-30 minutes or until a toothpick inserted into the center comes out clean.

8. Allow the cakes to cool completely.

For the Ice Cider Marzipan:
1. In a bowl, combine almond paste, powdered sugar, and high-end ice cider.

2. Knead the mixture until smooth and pliable.

3. Tint half of the marzipan with yellow food coloring until evenly colored.

For Assembly:
1. Roll out each color of marzipan separately into rectangles of the same size.

2. Warm apricot jam and brush it over one side of each cake.

3. Place the cakes side by side, one on top of the other, with the marzipan-covered sides facing each other.

4. Brush apricot jam over the top and sides of the assembled cakes.

5. Place the marzipan rectangles on the top and sides of the cakes, creating a checkerboard pattern.

6. Trim the excess marzipan to create clean edges.

Contemporary Ice Cider Recipes inspired by the Sweet Victorian Culinary Traditions

8. Raspberry Fool with Ice Cider Whipped Cream

The Raspberry Fool, a classic English dessert dating back centuries, has been cherished for its simplicity and delightful combination of fruit and cream. Our contemporary rendition pays homage to this timeless treat by introducing whipped cream infused with the nuanced sweetness of high-end ice cider, elevating the dessert to a new level of sophistication.

Indulge in the luscious experience of Raspberry Fool with Ice Cider Whipped Cream—a contemporary masterpiece that pays homage to the classic allure of this English dessert, now enriched by the subtle sweetness of high-end ice cider.

Ingredients:

- 2 cups fresh raspberries
- 1/2 cup granulated sugar
- 1 cup heavy cream
- 2 tablespoons high-end ice cider
- 1 teaspoon vanilla extract

Instructions:

1. In a blender or food processor, puree fresh raspberries until smooth.

2. Press the raspberry puree through a fine-mesh sieve to remove seeds, collecting the smooth raspberry sauce in a bowl.

3. In a separate bowl, whip heavy cream until soft peaks form.

4. Gently fold the raspberry sauce into the whipped cream.

5. Add granulated sugar, high-end ice cider, and vanilla extract to the mixture. Continue folding until well combined.

6. Spoon the Raspberry Fool into serving glasses or bowls.

7. Refrigerate for at least 2 hours to allow the flavors to meld.

Contemporary Ice Cider Recipes inspired by the Sweet Victorian Culinary Traditions

9. Custard Tart with Ice Cider Nutmeg

The Custard Tart, a staple in various culinary traditions, has graced tables for centuries. Our contemporary adaptation pays homage to this timeless treat by infusing the custard with the nuanced sweetness of high-end ice cider, adding a layer of complexity to the classic combination of custard and pastry. The addition of nutmeg harkens back to the historical use of this spice, symbolizing warmth and sophistication.

Ingredients:

For the Pastry:
- 1 1/4 cups all-purpose flour
- 1/2 cup unsalted butter, chilled and diced
- 1/4 cup granulated sugar
- 1 large egg yolk
- 2 tablespoons ice water

For the Custard Filling:
- 2 cups whole milk
- 1/2 cup granulated sugar
- 4 large egg yolks
- 2 tablespoons cornstarch
- 1/4 cup high-end ice cider
- 1 teaspoon vanilla extract
- 1/4 teaspoon ground nutmeg, plus extra for dusting

Instructions:
For the Pastry:

1. In a food processor, combine the all-purpose flour, chilled and diced unsalted butter, and granulated sugar. Pulse until the mixture resembles breadcrumbs.

2. Add the egg yolk and pulse until the dough comes together. If needed, add ice water one tablespoon at a time.

3. Turn the pastry out onto a floured surface and knead briefly to form a smooth ball.

4. Wrap the pastry in plastic wrap and refrigerate for at least 30 minutes.

For the Custard Filling:
1. In a saucepan, heat the whole milk until it just begins to simmer. Do not boil.

2. In a bowl, whisk together granulated sugar, egg yolks, and cornstarch until smooth.

3. Slowly pour the hot milk into the egg yolk mixture, whisking constantly.

4. Return the mixture to the saucepan and cook over medium heat, stirring constantly, until it thickens to a custard consistency.

5. Remove from heat and stir in the high-end ice cider, vanilla extract, and ground nutmeg. Allow the custard to cool to room temperature.

For Assembly:
1. Preheat the oven to 375°F (190°C). Grease a tart pan.

2. Roll out the chilled pastry on a floured surface to fit the tart pan.

3. Press the pastry into the pan and trim any excess.

4. Pour the cooled ice cider custard into the pastry shell.

5. Bake in the preheated oven for 25-30 minutes or until the custard is set and the pastry is golden brown.

6. Allow the Custard Tart to cool before dusting with additional ground nutmeg.

Contemporary Ice Cider Recipes inspired by the Sweet Victorian Culinary Traditions

10. Meringue Nests with Berries and Ice Cider Syrup

Meringue nests, celebrated for their light and airy texture, have been a dessert staple for generations. Our contemporary adaptation pays homage to this timeless treat by introducing a syrup infused with the nuanced sweetness of high-end ice cider. The result is a harmonious blend of crispy meringue, luscious berries, and a touch of sophisticated sweetness.

Ingredients:

- 4 large egg whites
- 1 cup granulated sugar
- 1 teaspoon white vinegar
- 1 teaspoon cornstarch
- 1 cup mixed fresh berries (strawberries, blueberries, raspberries)
- 2 tablespoons high-end ice cider
- 1 tablespoon powdered sugar (for dusting)

Instructions:

1. Preheat the oven to 250°F (120°C). Line a baking sheet with parchment paper.

2. In a clean, dry bowl, beat egg whites until soft peaks form.

3. Gradually add granulated sugar, one tablespoon at a time, while continuing to beat until stiff peaks form.

4. Gently fold in white vinegar and cornstarch until well combined.

5. Spoon the meringue mixture onto the prepared baking sheet, creating nests with a well in the center.

6. Bake in the preheated oven for 1.5 to 2 hours, or until the meringues are crisp on the outside.

7. Allow the meringue nests to cool completely.

8. In a small saucepan, combine high-end ice cider and mixed berries. Simmer over low heat until the berries release their juices and the mixture thickens slightly.

9. Spoon the berry mixture into the center of each meringue nest.

10. Dust with powdered sugar just before serving.

Indulge in the exquisite beauty of Meringue Nests with Ice Cider Syrup—a contemporary masterpiece that pays homage to the classic allure of meringue nests, now elevated by the nuanced sweetness of high-end ice cider.

Contemporary Ice Cider Recipes inspired by North American Cuisine

Welcome to a culinary journey where traditional North American recipes take on a new dimension of flavor and sophistication. In this collection, we reimagine classic dishes by infusing them with the rich and nuanced sweetness of high-quality ice cider. From savory delights to sweet indulgences, each recipe is a celebration of the bountiful harvest, where the crisp notes of ice cider enhance the culinary experience.

Savory Creations:

1. Maple Ice Cider Glazed Salmon:
Pan-seared salmon takes on a delightful twist with a glaze of maple syrup and ice cider, creating a symphony of sweet and tangy perfection.

2. Bourbon and Ice Cider BBQ Ribs:
Slow-cooked ribs, generously basted in a barbecue sauce infused with bourbon and ice cider, promise a tantalizing depth of flavor.

3. Ice Cider-Braised Short Ribs:
Short ribs undergo a luxurious transformation as they are braised in a flavorful broth featuring the subtle sweetness of ice cider.

4. Ice Cider-Glazed Bacon-Wrapped Shrimp:
Elevate your appetizer game with bacon-wrapped shrimp, glazed to perfection with a reduction of ice cider for a sweet and savory sensation.

5. Ice Cider-Infused Butternut Squash Soup:
Experience velvety butternut squash soup like never before, enriched with a drizzle of ice cider for a burst of natural sweetness.

6. Ice Cider-Glazed Brussels Sprouts with Pecans:
Roasted Brussels sprouts become a culinary delight when glazed with a reduction of ice cider and adorned with the crunch of toasted pecans.

7. Ice Cider-Chipotle BBQ Pulled Chicken Sliders:
Pulled chicken sliders take on a bold twist with a chipotle barbecue sauce sweetened to perfection with the addition of ice cider.

Sweeter Sensations:

8. Ice Cider Caramelized Onion Jam Crostini:
Indulge in creamy goat cheese atop crostini, crowned with a luscious caramelized onion jam sweetened with the complexity of ice cider.

9. Ice Cider-Maple Glazed Acorn Squash:
Roasted acorn squash reaches new heights with a glaze of maple syrup and ice cider, delivering a delightful side dish for any occasion.

10. Ice Cider-Pecan Stuffed Mushrooms:
Mushrooms stuffed with a savory blend of pecans and breadcrumbs find a touch of sweetness with the infusion of ice cider.

11. Ice Cider-Bacon Jam Breakfast Sandwich:
Kickstart your morning with a breakfast sandwich featuring bacon jam, where the sweetness of ice cider elevates every bite.

Contemporary Ice Cider Recipes inspired by North American Cuisine
1. Maple Ice Cider Glazed Salmon

Salmon, a revered staple in North American cuisine, has a profound connection to indigenous culinary traditions. Celebrating the rich tapestry of North American culinary history, this recipe honors the vital role of salmon in indigenous cultures. The addition of maple syrup, a timeless North American sweetener, and the nuanced sweetness of ice cider pays homage to the diverse and flavorful culinary legacy of the region.

Salmon, known for its various types, each with distinct flavors, textures, and characteristics, holds cultural significance in First Nations communities. Different salmon species are utilized in various ways, reflecting a deep understanding of the land and its resources.

This dish not only embodies the spirit of the land and its bounty but also introduces a contemporary flair that mirrors the evolution of North American gastronomy. Through the combination of traditional ingredients with a modern twist, this Maple Ice Cider Glazed Salmon offers a journey through time, celebrating the enduring connection between food, culture, and the evolving culinary landscape.

Ingredients:

- 4 salmon fillets
- Salt and pepper to taste
- 1/4 cup pure maple syrup
- 2 tablespoons high-quality ice cider
- 2 tablespoons olive oil
- Fresh dill for garnish

Instructions:

1. Season salmon fillets with salt and pepper.

2. In a bowl, mix maple syrup and ice cider to create the glaze.

3. Heat olive oil in a pan over medium-high heat.

4. Sear salmon fillets for 3-4 minutes on each side or until desired doneness.

5. Brush the glaze generously over the salmon during the last minute of cooking.

6. Transfer salmon to a serving platter, drizzle with any remaining glaze.

7. Garnish with fresh dill and serve immediately.

Contemporary Ice Cider Recipes inspired by North American Cuisine

2. Bourbon and Ice Cider BBQ Ribs

Barbecue, deeply embedded in North American culinary traditions, has evolved into a cultural phenomenon. Ribs, a quintessential barbecue delight, become a canvas for innovation with the addition of bourbon and ice cider. This modern twist pays homage to the rich history of barbecue while introducing a contemporary sophistication that reflects the ever-evolving palate of North American cuisine.

Ingredients:

- 2 racks of baby back ribs
- Salt and black pepper to taste
- 1 cup bourbon
- 1 cup high-quality ice cider
- 1 cup ketchup
- 1/2 cup brown sugar
- 1/4 cup apple cider vinegar
- 2 tablespoons Dijon mustard
- 1 tablespoon Worcestershire sauce
- 1 teaspoon smoked paprika
- 1 teaspoon garlic powder
- 1/2 teaspoon cayenne pepper (optional)

Instructions:

1. Preheat your grill or smoker to 225°F (107°C).

2. Season ribs with salt and black pepper.

3. In a saucepan, combine bourbon, ice cider, ketchup, brown sugar, apple cider vinegar, Dijon mustard, Worcestershire sauce, smoked paprika, garlic powder, and cayenne pepper (if using).

4. Bring the sauce to a simmer and cook for 15-20 minutes, allowing it to thicken.

5. Place the ribs on the grill and smoke for 3 hours.

6. Brush the ribs generously with the bourbon and ice cider barbecue sauce.

7. Continue smoking for an additional 30-60 minutes or until the ribs are tender.

8. Baste the ribs with more sauce before serving.

Indulge in the savory perfection of Bourbon and Ice Cider BBQ Ribs—a testament to the artistry of barbecue with a modern twist.

Contemporary Ice Cider Recipes inspired by North American Cuisine

3. Ice Cider-Braised Short Ribs

Braising, a cooking method embraced across culinary traditions, has deep roots in North American cuisine. Short ribs, prized for their rich marbling and depth of flavor, become a canvas for innovation with the infusion of ice cider. This modern adaptation pays homage to the timeless tradition of slow-cooked comfort foods while introducing a contemporary twist that reflects the evolving palate of North American gastronomy.

Ingredients:

- 4 lbs beef short ribs
- Salt and black pepper to taste
- 2 tablespoons vegetable oil
- 1 large onion, chopped
- 2 carrots, chopped
- 3 cloves garlic, minced
- 1 cup high-quality ice cider
- 2 cups beef broth
- 2 tablespoons tomato paste
- 2 sprigs fresh thyme
- 2 bay leaves

Instructions:

1. Preheat the oven to 325°F (163°C).

2. Season short ribs with salt and pepper.

3. Heat vegetable oil in a large, oven-safe pot over medium-high heat.

4. Brown short ribs on all sides and transfer to a plate.

5. In the same pot, sauté onion, carrots, and garlic until softened.

6. Stir in tomato paste and cook for 2 minutes.

7. Pour in ice cider, scraping up any browned bits from the bottom.

8. Return short ribs to the pot and add beef broth, thyme, and bay leaves.

9. Bring to a simmer, cover, and transfer to the preheated oven.

10. Braise for 2.5 to 3 hours or until the meat is fork-tender.

11. Remove thyme sprigs and bay leaves before serving.

Delight in the lusciousness of Ice Cider-Braised Short Ribs—a perfect union of tradition and innovation on your plate.

Contemporary Ice Cider Recipes inspired by North American Cuisine
4. Ice Cider-Glazed Bacon-Wrapped Shrimp

Bacon-wrapped delights have long been celebrated in North American cuisine, evolving from traditional practices to modern gastronomic delights. The addition of ice cider to the glaze brings a contemporary touch to this classic combination. This dish pays homage to the timeless appeal of bacon-wrapped treats while introducing a nuanced sweetness that reflects the evolving culinary landscape.

Ingredients:

- 1 lb large shrimp, peeled and deveined
- 1 lb bacon, cut in half
- Salt and black pepper to taste
- Wooden toothpicks, soaked in water
- 1 cup high-quality ice cider
- 1/4 cup brown sugar
- 1 teaspoon Dijon mustard
- 1/2 teaspoon garlic powder
- 1/4 teaspoon cayenne pepper (optional)

Instructions:

1. Preheat your oven to 375°F (190°C).

2. Season shrimp with salt and black pepper.

3. Wrap each shrimp with a half-slice of bacon and secure with a toothpick.

4. Place the wrapped shrimp on a baking sheet lined with parchment paper.

5. In a saucepan, combine ice cider, brown sugar, Dijon mustard, garlic powder, and cayenne pepper (if using).

6. Simmer the glaze over medium heat until it thickens slightly, about 10-12 minutes.

7. Brush the bacon-wrapped shrimp with the ice cider glaze.

8. Bake for 15-20 minutes or until the bacon is crispy and the shrimp are cooked through.

9. Baste with more glaze before serving.

Delight your guests with the exquisite flavors of Ice Cider-Glazed Bacon-Wrapped Shrimp—a sophisticated twist on a classic crowd-pleaser.

Contemporary Ice Cider Recipes inspired by North American Cuisine

5. Ice Cider-Infused Butternut Squash Soup

Squash soups have been a staple in North American kitchens, offering a canvas for creativity and seasonal exploration. The addition of ice cider to this classic butternut squash soup brings a modern twist, enhancing the natural sweetness of the squash with a nuanced fruity note. This dish pays homage to the enduring appeal of comforting soups while embracing the evolving taste preferences of contemporary cuisine.

Ingredients:

- 1 large butternut squash, peeled, seeded, and diced
- 1 onion, chopped
- 2 carrots, chopped
- 2 apples, peeled, cored, and chopped
- 3 cloves garlic, minced
- 4 cups vegetable broth
- 1 cup high-quality ice cider
- 1 teaspoon ground cinnamon
- 1/2 teaspoon ground nutmeg
- Salt and black pepper to taste
- Olive oil for cooking
- Fresh sage leaves for garnish (optional)

Instructions:

1. In a large pot, heat olive oil over medium heat.

2. Add chopped onion and garlic, sautéing until softened.

3. Add diced butternut squash, carrots, and apples to the pot. Cook for 5-7 minutes.

4. Pour in vegetable broth and ice cider. Bring to a simmer.

5. Season with ground cinnamon, ground nutmeg, salt, and black pepper.

6. Simmer for 20-25 minutes or until the vegetables are tender.

7. Use an immersion blender to puree the soup until smooth.

8. Adjust seasoning to taste.

9. Serve hot, garnished with fresh sage leaves if desired.

Savor the enchanting blend of flavors in Ice Cider-Infused Butternut Squash Soup—a delightful expression of seasonal comfort and contemporary culinary finesse.

Contemporary Ice Cider Recipes inspired by North American Cuisine
6. Ice Cider-Glazed Brussels Sprouts with Pecans

Brussels sprouts, once relegated to the sidelines, have undergone a remarkable renaissance, emerging as a star on contemporary menus. This resurgence reflects a shift in culinary preferences, with Brussels sprouts finding a new appreciation for their unique flavor and versatility. From humble beginnings to culinary stardom, these cruciferous delights showcase the dynamic evolution of North American cuisine.

The addition of ice cider to this classic Brussels sprouts dish introduces a touch of sophistication, elevating the vegetable to new culinary heights. This modern twist not only highlights the versatility of Brussels sprouts but also embraces the ever-evolving tastes of North American cuisine. As these once-overlooked greens take center stage, this recipe invites you to savor the perfect blend of tradition and innovation on your plate.

Ingredients:

- 1 lb Brussels sprouts, trimmed and halved
- 1/2 cup pecans, chopped
- 2 tablespoons olive oil
- Salt and black pepper to taste
- 1/2 cup high-quality ice cider
- 2 tablespoons maple syrup
- 1 tablespoon Dijon mustard

Instructions:

1. Preheat your oven to 400°F (200°C).

2. In a bowl, toss Brussels sprouts with olive oil, salt, and black pepper.

3. Spread the Brussels sprouts on a baking sheet in a single layer.

4. Roast in the preheated oven for 20-25 minutes or until golden brown and crispy on the edges.

5. In a small saucepan, combine ice cider, maple syrup, and Dijon mustard. Simmer over medium heat until the mixture thickens slightly.

6. Toast chopped pecans in a dry pan over medium heat until fragrant.

7. Drizzle the ice cider glaze over the roasted Brussels sprouts and toss to coat.

8. Sprinkle the glazed sprouts with toasted pecans.

9. Serve hot as a delectable side dish.

Contemporary Ice Cider Recipes inspired by North American Cuisine

7. Ice Cider-Chipotle BBQ Pulled Chicken Sliders

Pulled chicken sliders, beloved in North American cuisine, have undergone a fascinating transformation from classic barbecue fare to a platform for creative flavor exploration. Originating from traditional roots, these sliders have become a culinary canvas for inventive combinations. The contemporary twist in this recipe lies in the inclusion of ice cider in the chipotle BBQ sauce, symbolizing the continual journey of exploring bold and diverse flavors in modern North American cooking.

This dish encapsulates the dynamic evolution of culinary preferences, where cherished classics embrace new dimensions. The infusion of high-quality ice cider adds a layer of complexity, inviting you to experience the intersection of tradition and innovation with each delightful bite.

Ingredients:

- 2 lbs boneless, skinless chicken breasts
- 1 cup high-quality ice cider
- 1 cup tomato ketchup
- 1/4 cup apple cider vinegar
- 2 tablespoons chipotle peppers in adobo sauce, minced
- 2 tablespoons brown sugar
- 1 teaspoon smoked paprika
- 1 teaspoon garlic powder
- Salt and black pepper to taste
- Slider buns
- Coleslaw for topping (optional)

Instructions:

1. Place chicken breasts in a slow cooker.

2. In a bowl, whisk together ice cider, ketchup, apple cider vinegar, chipotle peppers, brown sugar, smoked paprika, garlic powder, salt, and black pepper.

3. Pour the sauce over the chicken in the slow cooker.

4. Cook on low for 6-8 hours or until the chicken is tender and easily shredded with a fork.

5. Shred the chicken using two forks and mix with the sauce.

6. Toast slider buns in the oven or on a skillet.

7. Spoon pulled chicken onto each slider bun.

8. Top with coleslaw if desired.

9. Serve hot Sliders.

Contemporary Ice Cider Recipes inspired by North American Cuisine
8. Ice Cider Caramelized Onion Jam Crostini

Caramelized onion jams boast a rich history, contributing depth and sweetness to diverse culinary creations. This timeless condiment has roots in traditional North American kitchens, where slow-cooked onions became a flavorful addition to a range of dishes. The infusion of ice cider in this recipe presents a modern twist, showcasing the ongoing evolution of classic flavor combinations in North American culinary traditions.

As culinary preferences continue to evolve, the addition of high-quality ice cider elevates the traditional caramelized onion jam, providing a nuanced and contemporary flavor profile. This recipe invites you to savor the intersection of history and innovation, capturing the essence of North American culinary heritage in each spoonful.

Ingredients:

- 2 large onions, thinly sliced
- 2 tablespoons olive oil
- 1/2 cup high-quality ice cider
- 2 tablespoons balsamic vinegar
- 1 tablespoon brown sugar
- Salt and black pepper to taste
- Baguette, sliced and toasted
- Goat cheese for spreading

Instructions:

1. Heat olive oil in a pan over medium-low heat.

2. Add sliced onions and cook, stirring occasionally, until softened and golden brown.

3. Pour in ice cider, balsamic vinegar, and brown sugar. Season with salt and black pepper.

4. Simmer over low heat until the liquid is reduced, and the onions have a jam-like consistency.

5. Allow the onion jam to cool slightly.

6. Spread goat cheese on toasted baguette slices.

7. Spoon a dollop of ice cider caramelized onion jam onto each crostini.

8. Arrange on a serving platter and enjoy this delightful appetizer.

Contemporary Ice Cider Recipes inspired by North American Cuisine

9. Ice Cider-Maple Glazed Acorn Squash

Acorn squash, a resilient and nutritious vegetable, has deep roots in North American culinary traditions. Indigenous peoples cultivated and celebrated squash long before the arrival of European settlers, emphasizing its significance in their diet through the "Three Sisters" agricultural system. European settlers adopted and adapted squash into their cuisine, and it became a staple in early American kitchens.

In the 19th and early 20th centuries, squash became a symbol of autumn abundance, featuring prominently in regional variations of dishes. Today, the Ice Cider-Maple Glazed Acorn Squash recipe honors this enduring legacy with a modern twist. The addition of high-quality ice cider elevates the classic roasted squash, infusing it with sophistication and connecting the past with contemporary culinary innovation. Enjoy a taste of history and innovation in every bite.

Ingredients:

- 2 acorn squash, halved and seeded
- 1/2 cup high-quality ice cider
- 1/4 cup maple syrup
- 2 tablespoons butter, melted
- 1 teaspoon cinnamon
- 1/2 teaspoon nutmeg
- Salt and black pepper to taste

Instructions:

1. Preheat your oven to 400°F (200°C).

2. Place acorn squash halves, cut side up, on a baking sheet.

3. In a bowl, whisk together ice cider, maple syrup, melted butter, cinnamon, nutmeg, salt, and black pepper.

4. Brush the glaze generously over each acorn squash half.

5. Roast in the preheated oven for 40-45 minutes or until the squash is tender and caramelized.

6. Baste the squash with the glaze halfway through the roasting time.

7. Remove from the oven and let it cool slightly.

8. Serve as a delightful side dish, allowing the flavors of Ice Cider-Maple Glazed Acorn Squash to complement your autumn feasts.

Celebrate the flavors of the season with this exquisite dish—a perfect balance of tradition and innovation, enriched by the addition of ice cider.

Contemporary Ice Cider Recipes inspired by North American Cuisine

10. Ice Cider-Pecan Stuffed Mushrooms

Stuffed mushrooms, a venerable appetizer dating back centuries, have been a canvas for culinary innovation across cultures. The concept of filling mushroom caps with flavorful mixtures has roots in both European and Asian cuisines. In North America, indigenous peoples were known to incorporate wild mushrooms into their traditional dishes.

As European settlers brought their culinary traditions to the New World, stuffed mushrooms evolved alongside the diverse bounty of the continent. The 19th century saw a surge in mushroom cultivation, and recipes for stuffed mushrooms gained popularity in Victorian-era cookbooks.

The late 20th and early 21st centuries witnessed a resurgence of interest in artisanal and locally-sourced ingredients. This culinary revival, coupled with an appreciation for craft beverages, has led to the integration of unique and high-quality elements in traditional recipes.

Our Ice Cider-Pecan Stuffed Mushrooms pay homage to this rich history by introducing a modern twist with the addition of high-quality ice cider. This sophisticated touch reflects the evolution of taste preferences and a commitment to elevating classic dishes, making them not just a culinary experience but a celebration of the cultural tapestry that defines North American cuisine.

Ingredients:

- 16 large mushrooms, stems removed and reserved
- 1/2 cup high-quality ice cider
- 1/2 cup breadcrumbs
- 1/4 cup finely chopped pecans
- 2 tablespoons olive oil
- 2 cloves garlic, minced
- 1 tablespoon fresh parsley, chopped
- Salt and black pepper to taste
- Grated Parmesan cheese for topping (optional)

Instructions:

1. Preheat your oven to 375°F (190°C).

2. Finely chop the mushroom stems.

3. In a skillet, heat olive oil over medium heat. Add chopped mushroom stems and garlic, sautéing until softened.

4. Pour in ice cider and simmer until most of the liquid has evaporated.

5. In a bowl, combine the sautéed mushroom mixture with breadcrumbs, chopped pecans, parsley, salt, and black pepper.

6. Stuff each mushroom cap with the prepared mixture.

7. Place the stuffed mushrooms on a baking sheet.

8. Bake in the preheated oven for 15-20 minutes or until the mushrooms are tender and the stuffing is golden brown.

9. Optionally, sprinkle with grated Parmesan cheese before serving.

Contemporary Ice Cider Recipes inspired by North American Cuisine

11. Ice Cider-Bacon Jam Breakfast Sandwich

The breakfast sandwich, a staple in many cultures, has undergone a fascinating transformation over the years. From humble beginnings in the 19th century as a portable and convenient meal for British workers, it has evolved into a global phenomenon. Bacon jam, with its sweet and savory allure, has become a contemporary favorite, embodying the spirit of modern North American breakfast traditions.

Ingredients:

- 4 English muffins, split and toasted
- 4 eggs, fried or scrambled
- 4 slices of your favorite cheese (cheddar, Swiss, or Gouda work well)
- 8 slices of bacon, cooked until crispy
- Ice Cider-Bacon Jam (see recipe below)

Ice Cider-Bacon Jam:
- 1 pound bacon, chopped
- 1 large onion, finely chopped
- 1/2 cup brown sugar
- 1/2 cup high-quality ice cider
- 1/4 cup apple cider vinegar
- 1 teaspoon Dijon mustard
- Salt and black pepper to taste

Instructions:

1. In a skillet, cook bacon until crispy. Remove excess fat, leaving about 2 tablespoons in the pan.

2. Add chopped onions to the bacon fat and cook until softened.

3. Stir in brown sugar, ice cider, apple cider vinegar, Dijon mustard, salt, and black pepper.

4. Simmer over low heat until the mixture thickens into a jam-like consistency.

5. Assemble the breakfast sandwich by placing a slice of cheese on the bottom half of each toasted English muffin.

6. Top with a fried or scrambled egg, two slices of crispy bacon, and a generous spoonful of Ice Cider-Bacon Jam.

7. Complete the sandwich with the other half of the toasted English muffin.

8. Serve immediately and savor the delightful combination of flavors in every bite.

Contemporary Ice Cider Recipes inspired by Pacific Rim Cuisine

Dive into the captivating world of Pacific Rim cuisine, a realm where the culinary traditions of Asia, Oceania, and the Americas intermingle to create an exquisite tapestry of flavors. In this chapter, we embark on a culinary exploration that marries the rich heritage of Pacific Rim dishes with the contemporary sophistication of ice cider, a luxurious addition that elevates the gastronomic experience to new heights.

Our journey begins with the Miso-Glazed Salmon, a dish that artfully balances the savory depth of miso with the subtle sweetness of ice cider reduction, resulting in a harmonious dance of flavors. Follow the trail to the Poke Bowl with Ice Cider Ponzu Sauce, where fresh tuna or salmon mingle with the zesty notes of ponzu, elevated by the infusion of ice cider.

For those seeking savory delights, the Soy-Ginger Ice Cider Chicken Skewers showcase the marriage of soy, ginger, and ice cider in a tantalizing marinade, transforming grilled chicken into a culinary masterpiece. The Lemongrass-Lime Ice Cider Shrimp, bathed in a fragrant blend of lemongrass, lime, and ice cider, offers a symphony of aromas and tastes, either grilled or sautéed to perfection.

In the realm of comfort, the Coconut Ice Cider Curry with Tofu emerges as a creamy and aromatic experience, with ice cider adding a nuanced sweetness to this delightful curry. The Wasabi-Sesame Ice Cider Edamame introduces a playful twist to the classic edamame, tossing it in a dressing that combines wasabi, sesame, and a drizzle of ice cider.

Turning our attention to the sweet finale, the Pineapple-Coconut Ice Cider Sorbet offers a refreshing tropical indulgence, highlighting the blend of pineapple, coconut, and the subtle sweetness of ice cider. Delight in the Coconut-Lemongrass Ice Cider Rice Pudding, a velvety dessert infused with coconut and lemongrass, sweetened with a touch of ice cider.

Conclude the culinary journey with the Dragon Fruit Ice Cider Cheesecake, where the vibrant hues of dragon fruit meet the delicate sweetness of ice cider in a dessert that's as visually stunning as it is delicious. The Sesame Ice Cider Cookies provide a crunchy and satisfying ending, with sesame seeds and a hint of ice cider creating a delightful bite.

Prepare to be transported to the crossroads of tradition and innovation as we reimagine Pacific Rim classics, infusing them with the elegance and complexity of ice cider. This chapter promises a fusion of flavors that transcends geographical boundaries, creating a culinary masterpiece that stands as a testament to the harmonious blend of timeless tradition and contemporary refinement.

Contemporary Ice Cider Recipes inspired by Pacific Rim Cuisine
1. Miso-Glazed Salmon with Ice Cider Reduction

The art of miso glazing can be traced back to ancient Japanese culinary traditions, where the umami-rich paste served as a key flavor enhancer. Miso, crafted from fermented soybeans, provided a depth of taste that became a cornerstone in Japanese cuisine. In this contemporary rendition, the infusion of ice cider pays homage to the evolution of North American gastronomy.

Ice cider, a product of innovative techniques and a nod to traditional apple cultivation, merges seamlessly with the miso glaze. This marriage of flavors transcends geographical boundaries, reflecting a culinary landscape that draws inspiration from diverse traditions. The result is a dish that not only showcases the time-honored techniques of Japan but also embraces the progressive spirit of modern North American cooking. As we celebrate the historical roots of miso glazing, we also acknowledge the dynamic fusion of global influences, making this Miso-Glazed Salmon a testament to the ever-evolving world of culinary arts.

Ingredients:

- 4 salmon fillets
- 1/4 cup miso paste
- 1/4 cup ice cider
- 2 tablespoons soy sauce
- 1 tablespoon mirin
- 1 tablespoon honey
- 1 teaspoon grated ginger
- Sesame seeds and sliced green onions for garnish

Instructions:

1. Preheat the grill to medium-high heat.

2. In a bowl, whisk together miso paste, ice cider, soy sauce, mirin, honey, and grated ginger to create the glaze.

3. Brush the salmon fillets with the miso and ice cider glaze, ensuring an even coating.

4. Grill the salmon for 4-5 minutes per side, or until it reaches your desired level of doneness.

5. Brush additional glaze during grilling for extra flavor.

6. Garnish with sesame seeds and sliced green onions.

7. Serve immediately and savor the exquisite balance of umami and sweetness in every bite.

Contemporary Ice Cider Recipes inspired by Pacific Rim Cuisine

2. Poke Bowl with Ice Cider Ponzu Sauce

The Poke Bowl with Ice Cider Ponzu Sauce transports you to the shores of the Pacific, drawing inspiration from the cherished culinary heritage of Hawaii. Historically, poke, meaning "to slice" in Hawaiian, traces its roots to the indigenous people of the islands who seasoned fresh, sliced fish with local ingredients.

Originally a simple dish, poke has evolved into a beloved culinary sensation, symbolizing the fusion of traditional flavors with contemporary creativity. In this recipe, fresh tuna or salmon takes center stage, paying homage to the historical significance of poke in native Hawaiian diets.

The Ice Cider Ponzu Sauce introduces a modern twist to the classic ponzu, which traditionally combines soy sauce, citrus, and mirin. Ice cider, with its sweet and fruity notes, enhances the ponzu, creating a zesty, nuanced drizzle that elevates the flavors of the poke bowl.

Immerse yourself in the culinary history of poke, where simplicity meets sophistication. This dish embodies the essence of Pacific Rim cuisine, blending the time-honored traditions of poke with the innovative touch of ice cider-infused ponzu. It's a celebration of heritage and contemporary culinary exploration in every vibrant, flavorful bite.

Ingredients:

- 1 lb fresh tuna or salmon, cubed
- 2 cups sushi rice, cooked
- 1 avocado, sliced
- 1 cucumber, julienned
- 1/4 cup green onions, chopped
- 1/4 cup sesame seeds
- 1/4 cup seaweed salad (optional)

For Ice Cider Ponzu Sauce:
- 1/4 cup soy sauce
- 2 tablespoons ice cider
- 1 tablespoon rice vinegar
- 1 tablespoon fresh lime juice
- 1 tablespoon mirin
- 1 teaspoon grated ginger
- 1 teaspoon honey
- 1 clove garlic, minced

Instructions:

1. In a bowl, whisk together all ingredients for the Ice Cider Ponzu Sauce.

2. In serving bowls, arrange sushi rice and top with cubed tuna or salmon.

3. Garnish with avocado slices, julienned cucumber, green onions, sesame seeds, and seaweed salad (if using).

4. Drizzle the Ice Cider Ponzu Sauce generously over the poke bowl.

5. Serve immediately, allowing the vibrant flavors to unfold with each delightful bite.

Contemporary Ice Cider Recipes inspired by Pacific Rim Cuisine
3.   Soy-Ginger Ice Cider Chicken Skewers

The Soy-Ginger Ice Cider Chicken Skewers present a harmonious blend of classic Asian flavors with a contemporary twist. Inspired by the time-honored combination of soy sauce and ginger in Asian cuisine, these skewers are elevated by the infusion of ice cider.

Historically, soy sauce and ginger have been fundamental components of Asian marinades, imparting depth and aromatic warmth to dishes. In this modern interpretation, the addition of ice cider introduces a subtle sweetness, creating a delightful balance of savory and sweet.

The Soy-Ginger Ice Cider Chicken Skewers embody the essence of Pacific Rim culinary traditions, where traditional ingredients meet innovative culinary exploration. Experience the succulence of grilled chicken, the richness of soy and ginger, and the nuanced sweetness contributed by ice cider. It's a journey into the heart of Pacific Rim flavors, blending heritage with a contemporary culinary perspective.

Ingredients:

- 1 lb chicken breast, cut into cubes
- 1/4 cup soy sauce
- 2 tablespoons ice cider
- 1 tablespoon sesame oil
- 1 tablespoon fresh ginger, grated
- 2 cloves garlic, minced
- 2 tablespoons green onions, chopped (for garnish)
- Sesame seeds (for garnish)

Instructions:

1. In a bowl, whisk together soy sauce, ice cider, sesame oil, grated ginger, and minced garlic to create the marinade.

2. Add the chicken cubes to the marinade, ensuring each piece is well-coated. Allow it to marinate for at least 30 minutes.

3. Preheat the grill or grill pan over medium-high heat.

4. Thread the marinated chicken cubes onto skewers.

5. Grill the skewers for 8-10 minutes, turning occasionally, until the chicken is cooked through and has a delightful char.

6. Garnish with chopped green onions and sesame seeds.

7. Serve the Soy-Ginger Ice Cider Chicken Skewers as a delectable appetizer or main course, capturing the essence of Pacific Rim cuisine with every flavorful bite.

Contemporary Ice Cider Recipes inspired by Pacific Rim Cuisine

4. Lemongrass-Lime Ice Cider Shrimp

The Lemongrass-Lime Ice Cider Shrimp is a delightful fusion of Pacific Rim flavors with a contemporary twist. Inspired by the fragrant combination of lemongrass and lime commonly found in Asian cuisine, this dish is elevated by the addition of ice cider.

Historically, lemongrass and lime have been key ingredients in Pacific Rim cooking, contributing citrusy and aromatic notes to various dishes. In this modern rendition, the infusion of ice cider introduces a layer of complexity, marrying traditional flavors with a touch of innovation.

The Lemongrass-Lime Ice Cider Shrimp invites you to experience the freshness of seafood, the aromatic blend of lemongrass and lime, and the unique sweetness brought by ice cider. It's a celebration of the diverse and evolving tastes found in the Pacific Rim, offering a contemporary culinary journey rooted in tradition.

Ingredients:

- 1 lb shrimp, peeled and deveined
- 2 tablespoons lemongrass, finely chopped
- Zest and juice of 1 lime
- 2 tablespoons ice cider
- 2 cloves garlic, minced
- 2 tablespoons fresh cilantro, chopped (for garnish)
- Salt and pepper to taste

Instructions:

1. In a bowl, combine finely chopped lemongrass, lime zest, lime juice, ice cider, minced garlic, salt, and pepper to create the marinade.

2. Add the peeled and deveined shrimp to the marinade, ensuring each shrimp is well-coated. Allow it to marinate for at least 20 minutes.

3. Heat a pan over medium-high heat.

4. Cook the marinated shrimp for 2-3 minutes on each side or until they turn pink and opaque.

5. Garnish with chopped fresh cilantro.

6. Serve the Lemongrass-Lime Ice Cider Shrimp over rice or as a standalone appetizer, savoring the exquisite blend of flavors that reflect the richness of Pacific Rim cuisine.

Contemporary Ice Cider Recipes inspired by Pacific Rim Cuisine

5. Coconut Ice Cider Curry with Tofu

The Coconut Ice Cider Curry with Tofu is a vibrant and contemporary twist on traditional Pacific Rim flavors. This dish draws inspiration from the rich culinary heritage of the region, combining creamy coconut curry with the subtle sweetness of ice cider.

Historically, coconut curry has been a staple in Pacific Rim cuisine, known for its velvety texture and aromatic spices. This modern adaptation introduces a touch of innovation by incorporating ice cider, elevating the dish with a nuanced sweetness.

The Coconut Ice Cider Curry with Tofu invites you to savor the harmonious blend of coconut richness, aromatic spices, and the delightful complexity of ice cider. It's a celebration of the diverse and evolving tastes found in the Pacific Rim, offering a contemporary experience that pays homage to traditional culinary roots.

Ingredients:

- 1 block extra-firm tofu, cubed
- 1 can (400 ml) coconut milk
- 2 tablespoons ice cider
- 2 tablespoons red curry paste
- 1 tablespoon soy sauce
- 1 tablespoon brown sugar
- 1 red bell pepper, sliced
- 1 cup broccoli florets
- Fresh cilantro for garnish
- Cooked jasmine rice for serving

Instructions:

1. In a large pan, combine coconut milk, ice cider, red curry paste, soy sauce, and brown sugar. Bring to a gentle simmer over medium heat.

2. Add cubed tofu, red bell pepper, and broccoli to the simmering curry. Cook until the vegetables are tender and the tofu has absorbed the flavors, stirring occasionally.

3. Taste and adjust the seasoning if needed.

4. Serve the Coconut Ice Cider Curry over jasmine rice, garnished with fresh cilantro.

5. Delight in the rich, creamy texture and complex flavors, appreciating the marriage of traditional Pacific Rim ingredients with the contemporary twist of ice cider.

6. Wasabi-Sesame Ice Cider Edamame

The Wasabi-Sesame Ice Cider *Edamame* dish is a fusion of traditional Japanese flavors and contemporary innovation, inspired by the diverse culinary landscape of the Pacific Rim. This unique creation combines the earthy freshness of *edamame* with the bold kick of *wasabi*, the nutty richness of sesame, and a modern twist of ice cider.

Historically, *edamame* has been a cherished snack in Japanese cuisine, celebrated for its vibrant green color and nutritional benefits. The addition of *wasabi* provides a zesty and aromatic element, while sesame adds a delightful nuttiness to the dish. The infusion of ice cider introduces a layer of sweetness, creating a balanced and sophisticated flavor profile.

This Pacific Rim-inspired dish pays homage to the traditional practice of enjoying *edamame* as a wholesome and flavorful snack. However, it elevates the experience by incorporating unexpected elements, reflecting the evolving tastes and creative exploration found in modern Pacific Rim cuisine.

The Wasabi-Sesame Ice Cider *Edamame* invites you to savor the contrast of flavors and textures—a delightful play between the heat of *wasabi*, the nuttiness of sesame, the natural freshness of *edamame*, and the subtle sweetness from the ice cider. It's a contemporary take on a classic snack, inviting you to embark on a culinary journey that bridges tradition and innovation.

Ingredients:

- 2 cups *edamame* (fresh or frozen)
- 2 tablespoons soy sauce
- 1 tablespoon ice cider
- 1 teaspoon sesame oil
- 1 teaspoon *wasabi* paste
- 1 tablespoon sesame seeds
- Sliced green onions for garnish

Instructions:

1. If using frozen *edamame*, cook according to package instructions. If using fresh, boil them until tender.

2. In a bowl, whisk together soy sauce, ice cider, sesame oil, and *wasabi* paste.

3. Toss the cooked *edamame* in the prepared sauce, ensuring they are well-coated.

4. Sprinkle sesame seeds over the *edamame* and toss again.

5. Garnish with sliced green onions before serving.

Contemporary Ice Cider Recipes inspired by Pacific Rim Cuisine
7. Pineapple-Coconut Ice Cider Sorbet

The Pineapple-Coconut Ice Cider Sorbet is a refreshing and tropical delight that draws inspiration from the Pacific Rim's vibrant and diverse culinary palette. This sorbet encapsulates the essence of tropical paradise with the sweet and tangy notes of pineapple, the creamy richness of coconut, and the contemporary twist of ice cider.

Historically, sorbets have been cherished for their ability to provide a palate-cleansing and refreshing experience. This Pacific Rim-inspired creation takes the concept of sorbet to new heights by incorporating flavors reminiscent of the lush landscapes and tropical fruits found in the region.

Pineapple, with its juicy sweetness, and coconut, known for its creamy texture, create a harmonious marriage of flavors in this sorbet. The addition of ice cider introduces a layer of complexity, enhancing the sweetness with its unique profile and contributing to the overall sophistication of the dessert.

This Pineapple-Coconut Ice Cider Sorbet embodies the spirit of the Pacific Rim's culinary traditions by blending familiar tropical tastes with a contemporary touch. It invites you to indulge in a frozen treat that not only refreshes the palate but also celebrates the exotic and diverse flavors of the Pacific Rim in a single, delightful scoop.

Ingredients:

- 2 cups fresh pineapple, chopped
- 1 cup coconut milk
- 1/2 cup ice cider
- 1/2 cup sugar
- Zest and juice of one lime

Instructions:

1. In a blender, combine fresh pineapple, coconut milk, ice cider, sugar, lime zest, and lime juice.

2. Blend until smooth and well combined.

3. Pour the mixture into an ice cream maker and churn according to the manufacturer's instructions.

4. Transfer the sorbet to a lidded container and freeze for at least 4 hours or until firm.

5. Scoop and serve the Pineapple-Coconut Ice Cider Sorbet in bowls or cones for a taste of tropical bliss.

Indulge in this Pineapple-Coconut Ice Cider Sorbet for a cool and exotic dessert experience that captures the allure of island flavors.

Contemporary Ice Cider Recipes inspired by Pacific Rim Cuisine
8. Coconut-Lemongrass Ice Cider Rice Pudding

The Coconut-Lemongrass Ice Cider Rice Pudding is a delectable fusion of traditional rice pudding with the aromatic flavors of coconut and lemongrass, inspired by the diverse and rich culinary traditions of the Pacific Rim. Rice pudding, a beloved dessert with variations found in many cultures, forms the canvas for this innovative creation that embraces the tropical essence of the Pacific Rim.

Historically, rice pudding has been a comforting and versatile treat enjoyed across the globe. In this Pacific Rim-inspired rendition, coconut and lemongrass take center stage, paying homage to the region's affinity for vibrant and aromatic ingredients. Coconut brings a creamy richness, while lemongrass imparts a citrusy and refreshing note, creating a harmonious blend that resonates with the Pacific Rim's culinary tapestry.

The addition of ice cider introduces a contemporary twist, elevating the dessert with its nuanced sweetness and complex undertones. Ice cider, known for its unique flavor profile, seamlessly integrates with the coconut and lemongrass, contributing a layer of sophistication to the rice pudding.

This dessert is a delightful exploration of Pacific Rim flavors, where traditional rice pudding meets the tropical allure of coconut and lemongrass, and the modern touch of ice cider adds a touch of elegance. It embodies the spirit of culinary innovation, inviting you to savor a fusion of timeless comfort and exotic sophistication.

Ingredients:

- 1 cup jasmine rice, rinsed
- 2 cups coconut milk
- 1/2 cup ice cider
- 1/2 cup sugar
- 2 stalks lemongrass, bruised
- Pinch of salt
- Toasted coconut flakes for garnish

Instructions:

1. In a saucepan, combine rinsed jasmine rice, coconut milk, ice cider, sugar, lemongrass, and a pinch of salt.

2. Bring the mixture to a simmer over medium heat, stirring occasionally.

3. Reduce the heat to low, cover, and let it simmer gently for 25-30 minutes or until the rice is tender.

4. Remove the lemongrass stalks and discard.

5. Let the rice pudding cool slightly before serving.

6. Garnish with toasted coconut flakes for added texture and flavor.

Contemporary Ice Cider Recipes inspired by Pacific Rim Cuisine

9. Dragon Fruit Ice Cider Cheesecake

The Dragon Fruit Ice Cider Cheesecake is a delightful homage to the tropical allure of dragon fruit, drawing inspiration from the vibrant and diverse culinary heritage of the Pacific Rim. Dragon fruit, with its exotic appearance and refreshing taste, has long been celebrated in Pacific Rim cuisine for its unique flavor profile and visual appeal.

In crafting this cheesecake, traditional elements of Pacific Rim desserts are thoughtfully incorporated, creating a fusion of timeless flavors and innovative techniques. The addition of ice cider represents a contemporary exploration of unique flavor profiles, seamlessly blending tradition with innovation. Ice cider, with its nuanced sweetness and complex notes, adds a layer of sophistication to the cheesecake, reflecting the evolving tastes and culinary experimentation that characterize modern Pacific Rim desserts.

This dessert captures the essence of the Pacific Rim's culinary journey—a harmonious blend of tradition and exploration, where the tropical flavors of dragon fruit and the modern twist of ice cider come together in a delightful celebration of the region's diverse and dynamic culinary landscape.

Ingredients:

- 2 cups graham cracker crumbs
- 1/2 cup unsalted butter, melted
- 24 oz cream cheese, softened
- 1 cup sugar
- 4 large eggs
- 1 teaspoon vanilla extract
- 1 cup dragon fruit puree
- 1/2 cup ice cider
- Dragon fruit slices for garnish

Instructions:

1. Preheat the oven to 325°F (163°C).

2. In a bowl, combine graham cracker crumbs and melted butter. Press the mixture into the base of a springform pan to form the crust.

3. In a large mixing bowl, beat cream cheese and sugar until smooth.

4. Add eggs one at a time, beating well after each addition. Stir in vanilla extract.

5. Pour in dragon fruit puree and ice cider, mixing until well combined.

6. Pour the batter over the crust in the springform pan.

7. Bake for 50-60 minutes or until the center is set.

8. Allow the cheesecake to cool completely before refrigerating for at least 4 hours or overnight.

9. Garnish with dragon fruit slices before serving.

Contemporary Ice Cider Recipes inspired by Pacific Rim Cuisine

10. Sesame Ice Cider Cookies

The Sesame Ice Cider Cookies draw inspiration from the rich and diverse culinary traditions that define the Pacific Rim. Sesame, a culinary staple in many Asian cuisines, has stood the test of time as an integral ingredient known for its distinctive nutty flavor and textural appeal. In these cookies, sesame takes center stage, paying homage to centuries-old culinary practices that have elevated this ingredient to a position of culinary reverence in the Pacific Rim.

The infusion of ice cider into the recipe marks a departure from tradition, introducing a contemporary twist that resonates with the evolving flavor preferences of modern Pacific Rim desserts. Ice cider, with its nuanced sweetness and complex notes, represents a nod to innovation and the integration of global influences into the culinary landscape. This infusion signifies the dynamic nature of Pacific Rim cuisine, where traditional ingredients meet contemporary tastes, resulting in a delightful fusion that captures the essence of culinary evolution in the region.

Ingredients:

- 1 cup unsalted butter, softened
- 1 cup sugar
- 1 large egg
- 1 teaspoon vanilla extract
- 2 cups all-purpose flour
- 1 cup sesame seeds
- 1/4 cup ice cider
- 1/2 teaspoon baking powder
- 1/4 teaspoon salt

Instructions:

1. Preheat the oven to 350°F (177°C) and line baking sheets with parchment paper.

2. In a large bowl, cream together butter and sugar until light and fluffy.

3. Beat in the egg and vanilla extract until well combined.

4. In a separate bowl, whisk together flour, sesame seeds, baking powder, and salt.

5. Gradually add the dry ingredients to the wet ingredients, mixing well.

6. Pour in the ice cider, continuing to mix until the dough comes together.

7. Scoop tablespoon-sized portions of dough and roll them into balls. Place them on the prepared baking sheets, leaving space between each.

8. Flatten each ball slightly with the back of a fork.

9. Bake for 12-15 minutes or until the edges are golden.

10. Allow the cookies to cool on the baking sheets for a few minutes before transferring them to a wire rack to cool completely.

Contemporary Ice Cider Recipes inspired by Chinese Cuisine

Embark on an extraordinary voyage through the heart of Chinese culinary artistry, where age-old traditions intertwine with contemporary elegance, creating a captivating symphony of flavors. In this chapter, titled "Harmony of Flavors: Ice Cider in Chinese Culinary Artistry," we extend a warm invitation to explore the rich tapestry of Chinese cuisine, now adorned with the nuanced notes of ice cider.

A unique cultural nuance accompanies our culinary exploration — in the intricacies of Chinese Mandarin, the number 13 radiates positive connotations, symbolizing 'assured growth' and 'definitely vibrant.' Embrace this auspicious energy as we delve into thirteen meticulously crafted recipes, each a celebration of China's vibrant culinary heritage.

Our culinary journey unfolds with the crisp delights of Peking Duck Tacos adorned with Ice Cider Hoisin Sauce, where traditional flavors meld seamlessly with the modern sweetness of ice cider. Traverse through the fiery landscapes of Szechuan Ice Cider Beef Stir-Fry, where each bite is a symphony of spicy notes harmonizing with the gentle sweetness of ice cider.

Transition into a realm of sweetness with the sophistication of Osmanthus Ice Cider Jelly, where delicate floral flavors are kissed by the gentle touch of ice cider. From the classic charm of Red Bean Ice Cider Mochi to the refreshing allure of Lychee Ice Cider Sorbet, each dessert is a culinary masterpiece, merging heritage with modernity.

Our exploration concludes with Mango-Coconut Ice Cider Sticky Rice, a delectable fusion of tropical flavors complemented by the subtlety of ice cider. The number 13, once considered ominous, now symbolizes a vibrant journey into a world where tradition and innovation coalesce.

So, whether you are an adept chef or a novice in the kitchen, "Harmony of Flavors" welcomes you to embrace the fusion of Chinese culinary artistry and the exquisite addition of ice cider. Revel in the symphony of tastes, celebrate the convergence of cultures, and craft memorable moments around your dining table. May your culinary voyage be marked by assured growth, vibrant experiences, and the delightful discovery of flavors both familiar and new.

Contemporary Ice Cider Recipes inspired by Chinese Cuisine

1. Peking Duck Tacos with Ice Cider Hoisin Sauce

Peking duck, a cherished dish with roots dating back to imperial China, has evolved into a symbol of culinary excellence. The delicate preparation of the duck, paired with the distinctive hoisin sauce, reflects the intricate balance of flavors in Chinese cuisine. The infusion of ice cider into the hoisin sauce brings a contemporary twist, paying homage to the rich history of Peking duck while embracing the evolving palate of modern gastronomy.

Ingredients:

- Peking duck, thinly sliced
- Mini flour tortillas
- Ice cider hoisin sauce (see below)
- Fresh cucumber, julienned
- Green onions, chopped

Ice Cider Hoisin Sauce:
- 1/2 cup hoisin sauce
- 2 tablespoons ice cider
- 1 tablespoon soy sauce
- 1 tablespoon rice vinegar
- 1 teaspoon sesame oil

Instructions:

1. Prepare the Ice Cider Hoisin Sauce:
  - In a bowl, whisk together hoisin sauce, ice cider, soy sauce, rice vinegar, and sesame oil until well combined.

2. Assemble the Tacos:
   - Warm the mini flour tortillas.
   - Place a few slices of Peking duck on each tortilla.
   - Drizzle with the ice cider hoisin sauce.
   - Top with julienned cucumber and chopped green onions.

3. Serve and Enjoy:
   - Arrange the Peking Duck Tacos on a serving platter.
   - Serve immediately and savor the harmonious blend of flavors.

Contemporary Ice Cider Recipes inspired by Chinese Cuisine

2. Szechuan Ice Cider Beef Stir-Fry

Szechuan cuisine, renowned for its bold and spicy flavors, has a rich history dating back to ancient China. The use of Szechuan peppercorns contributes a distinctive numbing heat to the stir-fry, showcasing the region's culinary prowess. The infusion of ice cider into the sauce introduces a contemporary touch, harmonizing tradition and innovation in a single, exhilarating dish.

Ingredients:
- 1 lb beef sirloin, thinly sliced
- 2 tablespoons vegetable oil
- 1 tablespoon Szechuan peppercorns
- 1 red bell pepper, sliced
- 1 yellow bell pepper, sliced
- 1 cup snow peas, ends trimmed
- 4 green onions, chopped

Ice Cider Stir-Fry Sauce:
- 1/4 cup soy sauce
- 2 tablespoons ice cider
- 1 tablespoon hoisin sauce
- 1 tablespoon rice vinegar
- 1 tablespoon brown sugar
- 1 teaspoon sesame oil
- 2 cloves garlic, minced
- 1 tablespoon fresh ginger, grated
- 1 tablespoon cornstarch

Instructions:

1. Prepare the Ice Cider Stir-Fry Sauce:
   - In a bowl, whisk together soy sauce, ice cider, hoisin sauce, rice vinegar, brown sugar, sesame oil, minced garlic, grated ginger, and cornstarch. Set aside.

2. Stir-Fry the Beef:
   - Heat vegetable oil in a wok or large skillet over high heat.
   - Add Szechuan peppercorns and stir-fry for 30 seconds.
   - Add sliced beef and cook until browned. Remove beef from the wok and set aside.

3. Stir-Fry the Vegetables:
   - In the same wok, add more oil if needed.
   - Stir-fry bell peppers and snow peas until crisp-tender.

4. Combine and Finish:
   - Return the cooked beef to the wok.
   - Pour the ice cider stir-fry sauce over the beef and vegetables.
   - Stir-fry until the sauce thickens and coats the ingredients.

5. Serve and Enjoy:
   - Garnish with chopped green onions.
   - Serve the Szechuan Ice Cider Beef Stir-Fry over rice or noodles.

Contemporary Ice Cider Recipes inspired by Chinese Cuisine
3. General Tso's Ice Cider Chicken Wings

General Tso's Chicken, a popular Chinese-American dish, traces its roots to the Hunan province of China. The tangy and spicy sauce traditionally coats deep-fried chicken, creating a symphony of flavors. Adding ice cider to the sauce provides a contemporary touch, imparting a nuanced sweetness that complements the dish's bold profile.

Ingredients:

- 2 lbs chicken wings
- Vegetable oil, for frying
- Sesame seeds and chopped green onions for garnish

For the Ice Cider General Tso's Sauce:
- 1/2 cup ice cider
- 1/4 cup soy sauce
- 3 tablespoons hoisin sauce
- 3 tablespoons rice vinegar
- 3 tablespoons honey
- 2 tablespoons ketchup
- 2 cloves garlic, minced
- 1 tablespoon fresh ginger, grated
- 1 teaspoon sesame oil
- 1 teaspoon cornstarch (optional, for thickening)

Instructions:

1. Fry the Chicken Wings:
   - Heat vegetable oil in a deep fryer or large pot to 375°F (190°C).
   - Fry chicken wings until golden brown and crispy. Drain on paper towels.

2. Prepare the Ice Cider General Tso's Sauce:
   - In a saucepan, combine ice cider, soy sauce, hoisin sauce, rice vinegar, honey, ketchup, minced garlic, grated ginger, and sesame oil.
   - If desired, mix cornstarch with a tablespoon of water and add to the sauce for thickening.
   - Simmer over medium heat until the sauce thickens.

3. Coat the Chicken Wings:
   - In a large bowl, toss the fried chicken wings with the ice cider General Tso's sauce until evenly coated.

4. Garnish and Serve:
   - Arrange the coated wings on a serving platter.
   - Garnish with sesame seeds and chopped green onions.

5. Enjoy:
   - Dive into the irresistible fusion of crispy chicken wings and the distinctive flavors of General Tso's Ice Cider Chicken Wings.

Savor the delectable balance of sweet and spicy in this innovative take on a classic Chinese-American favorite. These wings are sure to be a hit at any gathering, combining tradition with a contemporary twist.

Contemporary Ice Cider Recipes inspired by Chinese Cuisine

4. Five-Spice Ice Cider Glazed Ribs

These ribs are a showstopper, marrying the time-honored essence of five-spice with the contemporary touch of ice cider, resulting in a flavor experience that transcends culinary boundaries.

Five-spice powder, a cornerstone of Chinese cuisine, typically consists of star anise, cloves, Chinese cinnamon, Sichuan pepper, and fennel seeds. This blend imparts a robust and fragrant profile to many Chinese dishes. Introducing ice cider into the glaze not only adds a layer of sweetness but also showcases the adaptability of ancient flavors in modern gastronomy.

Ingredients:

- 2 racks of baby back ribs
- Salt and black pepper, to taste
- Sesame seeds and chopped green onions for garnish

For the Five-Spice Ice Cider Glaze:
- 1 cup ice cider
- 1/4 cup soy sauce
- 3 tablespoons honey
- 1 tablespoon hoisin sauce
- 1 teaspoon Chinese five-spice powder
- 2 cloves garlic, minced
- 1 tablespoon fresh ginger, grated
- 1 tablespoon sesame oil

Instructions:

1. Preheat the Oven:
   - Preheat your oven to 275°F (135°C).

2. Prepare the Ribs:
   - Remove the membrane from the back of the ribs and season with salt and black pepper.

3. Slow Roast the Ribs:
   - Place the seasoned ribs on a baking sheet and slow roast in the preheated oven for 2.5 to 3 hours until tender.

4. Make the Five-Spice Ice Cider Glaze:
   - In a saucepan, combine ice cider, soy sauce, honey, hoisin sauce, Chinese five-spice powder, minced garlic, grated ginger, and sesame oil.
   - Simmer the mixture over medium heat until it thickens into a glaze.

5. Glaze the Ribs:
   - Brush the roasted ribs generously with the Five-Spice Ice Cider Glaze.

6. Broil for Caramelization:
   - Set your oven to broil and place the glazed ribs under the broiler for 3-5 minutes, or until caramelized.

7. Garnish and Serve:
   - Sprinkle sesame seeds and chopped green onions over the glazed ribs.

Contemporary Ice Cider Recipes inspired by Chinese Cuisine

5. Dim Sum Ice Cider Dumplings

Dim sum, a treasured culinary tradition, traces its origins to the teahouses along the Silk Road. These delectable bite-sized treats have evolved over centuries, with each dumpling representing a unique regional influence. The addition of ice cider to the sauce showcases the adaptability of Chinese culinary heritage to contemporary tastes.

Ingredients:

- 1 package round dumpling wrappers
- 1/2 pound ground pork
- 1/2 pound shrimp, peeled and deveined, finely chopped
- 2 green onions, finely chopped
- 2 tablespoons soy sauce
- 1 tablespoon oyster sauce
- 1 tablespoon ice cider
- 1 teaspoon sesame oil
- 1 teaspoon fresh ginger, grated
- 1/2 teaspoon sugar
- Pinch of white pepper
- Water (for sealing dumplings)

Instructions:

1. Prepare the Filling:
   - In a bowl, combine ground pork, chopped shrimp, green onions, soy sauce, oyster sauce, ice cider, sesame oil, grated ginger, sugar, and white pepper. Mix thoroughly.

2. Assemble the Dumplings:
   - Place a small amount of filling in the center of a dumpling wrapper.
   - Moisten the edge of the wrapper with water, fold in half, and press to seal, creating a half-moon shape.
   - Pleat the edges for a decorative touch.

3. Steam the Dumplings:
   - Arrange the dumplings on a steamer lined with parchment paper.
   - Steam for 12-15 minutes until the dumplings are cooked through.

4. Serve and Enjoy:
   - Plate the Dim Sum Ice Cider Dumplings and savor the combination of traditional flavors and the subtle sweetness of ice cider.

Elevate your dim sum experience with these exquisite dumplings, showcasing the seamless integration of classic techniques and the contemporary sophistication of ice cider. Each bite is a testament to the culinary artistry that defines Chinese gastronomy.

Contemporary Ice Cider Recipes inspired by Chinese Cuisine

6. Red Bean Ice Cider Mochi

Mochi, a traditional Japanese treat, has been savored for centuries, often associated with celebrations and festive occasions. Red bean paste, known as "anko" in Japanese, is a staple in many sweets and desserts. The addition of ice cider introduces a modern twist, highlighting the evolution of traditional Japanese flavors.

Ingredients:

- 1 cup sweet rice flour (mochiko)
- 1/4 cup sugar
- 1 cup water
- Cornstarch (for dusting)
- Red bean paste (store-bought or homemade)
- Ice cider

Instructions:

1. Prepare the Mochi Dough:
   - In a heatproof bowl, whisk together sweet rice flour, sugar, and water until smooth.
   - Cover the bowl loosely with plastic wrap and microwave for 2-3 minutes until the mixture becomes translucent, stirring every minute.

2. Shape the Mochi:
   - Dust a clean surface with cornstarch.
   - Transfer the mochi dough to the surface and divide it into small portions.
   - Flatten each portion, place a small amount of red bean paste in the center, and encase the paste with the mochi dough.

3. Seal and Chill:
   - Pinch and seal the edges of the mochi to create a ball or disc shape.
   - Place the mochi on a plate dusted with cornstarch and refrigerate for about 30 minutes.

4. Serve with Ice Cider Drizzle:
   - Drizzle a bit of ice cider over the chilled Red Bean Ice Cider Mochi before serving.

5. Enjoy the Delightful Treat:
   - Relish the soft and chewy texture of the mochi complemented by the sweet richness of red bean paste, all elevated with a touch of ice cider.

Celebrate the union of tradition and innovation with Red Bean Ice Cider Mochi, a testament to the artistry of Japanese sweets. Each bite encapsulates the essence of cultural heritage infused with a contemporary flair.

Contemporary Ice Cider Recipes inspired by Chinese Cuisine

7. Lychee Ice Cider Sorbet

Lychee, a tropical fruit cherished for its fragrant and sweet taste, has been enjoyed for centuries in various Asian cuisines. This sorbet pays homage to the rich tradition of incorporating lychee into desserts. The infusion of ice cider introduces a contemporary touch, reflecting the evolving palate of modern gastronomy.

Ingredients:

- 2 cups fresh or canned lychee, drained
- 1/2 cup sugar
- 1/4 cup ice cider
- 1 tablespoon fresh lime juice

Instructions:

1. Prepare the Lychee Puree:
   - In a blender, combine lychee, sugar, ice cider, and lime juice.
   - Blend until smooth to create a lychee puree.

2. Chill the Mixture:
   - Transfer the lychee puree to a bowl and refrigerate for at least 2 hours to chill the mixture thoroughly.

3. Freeze in Ice Cream Maker:
   - Pour the chilled lychee mixture into an ice cream maker.
   - Churn according to the manufacturer's instructions until the sorbet reaches a soft, frozen consistency.

4. Transfer and Freeze:
   - Transfer the sorbet to a lidded container and freeze for an additional 2-4 hours or until firm.

5. Serve and Enjoy:
   - Scoop the Lychee Ice Cider Sorbet into bowls or cones.
   - Garnish with fresh lychee or a drizzle of ice cider if desired.

8. Hong Kong-Style Egg Custard Tart with Ice Cider Glaze

Egg custard tarts, a hallmark of Hong Kong dim sum, boast a rich history rooted in Chinese culinary heritage. This recipe honors that legacy while introducing a contemporary twist through the addition of an ice cider glaze. The result is a dessert that seamlessly melds tradition with innovation.

Ingredients:

For the Pastry:
- 1 1/2 cups all-purpose flour
- 1/2 cup unsalted butter, chilled and cubed
- 2 tablespoons sugar
- 1 egg yolk
- 2 tablespoons ice water

For the Custard Filling:
- 4 large eggs
- 1/2 cup sugar
- 1 1/2 cups whole milk
- 1 teaspoon vanilla extract

For the Ice Cider Glaze:
- 1/4 cup ice cider
- 2 tablespoons apricot preserves

Instructions:

1. Prepare the Pastry:
   - In a food processor, combine flour, butter, and sugar. Pulse until the mixture resembles coarse crumbs.
   - Add the egg yolk and ice water. Pulse until the dough comes together.
   - Shape the dough into a disk, wrap in plastic, and chill for at least 30 minutes.

2. Roll Out the Dough:
   - Preheat the oven to 375°F (190°C).
   - Roll out the chilled dough on a floured surface and line tart molds or a muffin tin.

3. Prepare the Custard Filling:
   - In a bowl, whisk together eggs, sugar, milk, and vanilla until well combined.
   - Pour the custard mixture into the prepared tart shells.

4. Bake:
   - Bake for 15-20 minutes or until the custard is set and the pastry is golden brown.

5. Make the Ice Cider Glaze:
   - In a small saucepan, heat ice cider and apricot preserves over low heat until combined. Allow the glaze to cool.

6. Glaze the Tarts:
   - Once the tarts are cool, brush the tops with the ice cider glaze.

7. Chill and Serve:
   - Chill the tarts in the refrigerator for at least 1 hour before serving.

Indulge in the exquisite blend of velvety custard and the subtle sweetness of the Ice Cider Glaze—a Hong Kong-style treat that captures the essence of time-honored dim sum with a modern flair.

Contemporary Ice Cider Recipes inspired by Chinese Cuisine

9. Pineapple Ice Cider Buns

Buns, a staple in Chinese cuisine, symbolize prosperity and wealth. Our Pineapple Ice Cider Buns pay homage to this tradition while incorporating the contemporary touch of ice cider. Pineapple, a symbol of luck, further enriches the cultural significance of this delectable treat.

Ingredients:
For the Dough:

- 2 1/4 teaspoons active dry yeast
- 1 cup warm milk
- 1/4 cup sugar
- 3 cups all-purpose flour
- 1/4 cup unsalted butter, softened
- 1/2 teaspoon salt

For the Pineapple Filling:
- 1 cup crushed pineapple, drained
- 1/4 cup sugar
- 2 tablespoons cornstarch

For the Ice Cider Glaze:
- 1/3 cup ice cider
- 2 tablespoons powdered sugar

Instructions:

1. Activate the Yeast:
   - In a bowl, combine warm milk, sugar, and yeast. Let it sit for 5-10 minutes until frothy.

2. Make the Dough:
   - In a large bowl, mix flour, softened butter, and salt. Add the activated yeast mixture and knead until a smooth dough forms.
   - Cover the bowl and let the dough rise in a warm place until doubled in size.

3. Prepare the Pineapple Filling:
   - In a saucepan, combine crushed pineapple, sugar, and cornstarch. Cook over medium heat until thickened. Allow it to cool.

4. Form the Buns:
   - Punch down the risen dough and divide it into small portions. Flatten each portion and add a spoonful of pineapple filling. Seal the edges to form buns.

5. Second Rise:
   - Place the buns on a baking sheet and let them rise for another 30-40 minutes.

6. Bake:
   - Preheat the oven to 350°F (180°C). Bake the buns for 15-20 minutes or until golden brown.

7. Make the Ice Cider Glaze:
   - In a small bowl, whisk together ice cider and powdered sugar until smooth.

8. Glaze the Buns:
   - Once the buns are cool, drizzle the ice cider glaze over the top.

Savor the marriage of pineapple-infused bliss and the subtle sweetness of the Ice Cider Glaze in each soft, aromatic Pineapple Ice Cider Bun—a delightful fusion of tradition and innovation.

Contemporary Ice Cider Recipes inspired by Chinese Cuisine
10. Jasmine Tea-Ice Cider Panna Cotta

Panna Cotta, meaning "cooked cream" in Italian, has a rich history in European culinary traditions. Our version takes inspiration from this classic dessert and infuses it with the aromatic essence of jasmine tea, a symbol of purity and grace in Chinese culture. The addition of ice cider elevates this dish, highlighting the seamless blend of diverse flavors.

Ingredients:

- 1 cup whole milk
- 1 tablespoon jasmine tea leaves
- 2 teaspoons unflavored gelatin
- 2 tablespoons cold water
- 2 cups heavy cream
- 1/2 cup sugar
- 1/2 cup ice cider
- 1 teaspoon vanilla extract

Instructions:

1. Infuse the Milk:
   - In a saucepan, heat the whole milk until it's just about to simmer. Remove from heat and add jasmine tea leaves. Let it steep for 10-15 minutes. Strain out the tea leaves.

2. Bloom the Gelatin:
   - In a small bowl, sprinkle gelatin over cold water. Allow it to bloom for 5 minutes.

3. Prepare the Panna Cotta Mixture:
   - In a clean saucepan, combine the infused milk, heavy cream, and sugar. Warm the mixture over medium heat until it's about to boil. Remove from heat.
   - Add the bloomed gelatin to the warm mixture and stir until completely dissolved.
   - Stir in the ice cider and vanilla extract.

4. Pour into Molds:
   - Divide the mixture among serving glasses or molds.

5. Chill:
   - Refrigerate the panna cotta for at least 4 hours or until set.

6. Serve:
   - Once set, serve the Jasmine Tea-Ice Cider Panna Cotta chilled, either in the molds or unmolded onto plates.

Relish the ethereal essence of jasmine tea and the refined sweetness of ice cider in each silky spoonful of this Jasmine Tea-Ice Cider Panna Cotta—a testament to the artful fusion of cultures and flavors.

Contemporary Ice Cider Recipes inspired by Chinese Cuisine

11. Sesame Ginger Ice Cider Parfait

Sesame and ginger are staples in Chinese cuisine, celebrated for their diverse applications in both savory and sweet dishes. This parfait pays homage to these traditional flavors, while the addition of ice cider brings a modern twist, symbolizing the ongoing evolution of Chinese culinary traditions.

Ingredients:

- 1 cup heavy cream
- 2 tablespoons powdered sugar
- 1 teaspoon vanilla extract
- 2 tablespoons sesame seeds, toasted
- 2 tablespoons crystallized ginger, finely chopped
- 1/4 cup ice cider

Instructions:

1. Whip the Cream:
   - In a chilled bowl, whip the heavy cream until soft peaks form.
   - Add powdered sugar and vanilla extract. Continue whipping until stiff peaks form.

2. Prepare Sesame Ginger Mixture:
   - In a separate bowl, combine toasted sesame seeds and finely chopped crystallized ginger.

3. Layering:
   - In serving glasses, alternate layers of whipped cream and the sesame ginger mixture.

4. Drizzle with Ice Cider:
   - Before serving, drizzle each parfait with a splash of ice cider.

5. Garnish:
   - Optionally, garnish with additional toasted sesame seeds and crystallized ginger.

6. Serve:
   - Serve the Sesame Ginger Ice Cider Parfait immediately and enjoy the delightful interplay of flavors and textures.

Indulge in this Sesame Ginger Ice Cider Parfait as a delightful conclusion to your meal, savoring the marriage of traditional Chinese ingredients with the contemporary flair of ice cider.

Contemporary Ice Cider Recipes inspired by Chinese Cuisine
12. Mango-Coconut Ice Cider Sticky Rice

Sticky rice, or glutinous rice, has been a culinary cornerstone in Asian cultures for centuries, its roots entwined with the rich tapestry of traditions and customs. Originating in East and Southeast Asia, this unique variety of rice earned its moniker for its sticky and glutinous texture, which plays a pivotal role in a myriad of traditional dishes.

In the realm of desserts, sticky rice is a revered ingredient, celebrated for its ability to transform into delectable, chewy treats. Chinese cuisine, in particular, boasts a long history of crafting intricate and flavorful desserts with sticky rice, often symbolizing unity, prosperity, and familial bonds.

The Mango-Coconut Ice Cider Sticky Rice pays homage to this storied tradition, drawing inspiration from the artistry of crafting sweet delights with glutinous rice. The infusion of ice cider, a modern and sophisticated twist, reflects the evolving landscape of Chinese culinary practices, where traditional recipes seamlessly integrate with contemporary elements.

As Chinese gastronomy continues to embrace innovation while honoring its heritage, this dessert stands as a testament to the enduring appeal of sticky rice desserts and the delightful surprises that come with the infusion of new flavors, in this case, the nuanced sweetness of ice cider. Through each spoonful, savor not just the flavors but the journey through time and cultural heritage, encapsulated in the humble yet profound sticky rice dessert.

Ingredients:

- 1 cup glutinous rice, soaked for at least 4 hours or overnight
- 1 cup coconut milk
- 1/4 cup ice cider
- 2 tablespoons sugar
- 1/2 teaspoon salt
- Ripe mango, peeled, pitted, and sliced for serving

Instructions:

1. Steam the Sticky Rice:
   - Drain the soaked glutinous rice and steam it until tender, approximately 20-25 minutes.

2. Prepare Coconut Sauce:
   - In a saucepan, heat coconut milk, ice cider, sugar, and salt over medium heat. Stir until the sugar dissolves.

3. Combine Sticky Rice and Coconut Sauce:
   - Transfer the steamed sticky rice to a large bowl.
   - Pour the warm coconut sauce over the rice and gently fold until well combined.

4. Let it Rest:
   - Allow the sticky rice to rest for 15-20 minutes to absorb the flavors.

5. Serve:
   - Spoon the Mango-Coconut Ice Cider Sticky Rice onto serving plates or bowls.
   - Top with slices of ripe mango.

6. Drizzle with More Ice Cider:
   - Before serving, drizzle a bit more ice cider over the dessert for an extra layer of sweetness.

Contemporary Ice Cider Recipes inspired by Chinese Cuisine
13. Osmanthus Ice Cider Jelly

In Chinese culture, the *osmanthus* flower is not merely a botanical marvel; it is a revered symbol of beauty, grace, and the transient nature of life. For centuries, the delicate fragrance of *osmanthus* blossoms has graced Chinese gardens, permeating the air with a sweet and intoxicating aroma. As an enduring emblem of purity and elegance, *osmanthus* has found its place in art, poetry, and, of course, culinary traditions.

The *Osmanthus* Ice Cider Jelly pays homage to this rich cultural legacy, fusing the timeless allure of *osmanthus* with a contemporary twist—ice cider. This floral-infused jelly becomes a canvas where tradition meets innovation, embodying the essence of Chinese culinary history.

As you savor each spoonful of this delicate dessert, you are transported through time, experiencing the harmonious blend of fragrant *osmanthus* and the subtle sweetness of ice cider. In Chinese culinary philosophy, where flavors are intertwined with cultural symbolism, this dessert becomes a celebration of beauty, continuity, and the ever-evolving nature of Chinese gastronomy. Embrace the intricate tapestry of Chinese history with every delightful, floral-infused bite, a testament to the enduring charm of *osmanthus* and the innovative spirit of Chinese culinary traditions.

Ingredients:

- 1/4 cup dried *osmanthus* flowers
- 1 cup water
- 1 cup ice cider
- 1/4 cup honey
- 2 tablespoons agar-agar powder

Instructions:

1. Prepare Osmanthus Infusion:
   - In a saucepan, bring 1 cup of water to a gentle simmer.
   - Add dried osmanthus flowers and let them steep for 10-15 minutes.
   - Strain the osmanthus infusion, discarding the flowers.

2. Create Ice Cider-Honey Mixture:
   - In a separate bowl, mix ice cider and honey until well combined.

3. Combine *Osmanthus* Infusion and Ice Cider Mixture:
   - Pour the *osmanthus* infusion into the ice cider-honey mixture, stirring to blend the flavors.

4. Activate Agar-Agar:
   - In a clean saucepan, sprinkle agar-agar powder over the liquid mixture.
   - Let it sit for a few minutes to activate the agar-agar.

5. Simmer and Stir:
   - Gently heat the mixture over medium heat, stirring constantly until the agar-agar dissolves completely.

6. Bring to a Boil:
   - Increase the heat and bring the mixture to a boil. Allow it to boil for 1-2 minutes.

7. Set in Molds:
   - Pour the liquid jelly into molds or serving glasses.

8. Chill:
   - Refrigerate the jelly for at least 2 hours or until fully set.

9. Serve:
   - Once set, unmold the *Osmanthus* Ice Cider Jelly or serve it in glasses.

Two Cocktails

Ice Cider Spiked New York Sour

The New York Sour, a classic cocktail, traces its roots to the vibrant and eclectic cocktail culture of New York City. As an homage to this iconic concoction, we present a modern twist inspired by the renowned mixologist Dale DeGroff.

In the heart of the city that never sleeps, the New York Sour has become a symbol of sophistication and indulgence. Its layered presentation, with a red wine float atop a whiskey sour base, reflects the city's dynamic and multifaceted character.

Recipe:

Ingredients:
- 2 oz bourbon
- 1 oz simple syrup
- 1 oz fresh lemon juice
- 1/2 oz red wine
- Ice cider for float

Instructions:
1. In a shaker, combine bourbon, simple syrup, and fresh lemon juice.
2. Fill the shaker with ice and shake vigorously.
3. Strain the mixture into a rocks glass filled with ice.
4. Gently pour red wine over the back of a spoon to create a float on top of the cocktail.
5. Finish by adding a float of ice cider on top.

Serving Notes:
The addition of ice cider elevates this classic cocktail, introducing a nuanced layer of sweetness and complexity. Sip and savor the fusion of tradition and innovation, a toast to the ever-evolving cocktail culture that defines the spirit of New York City.

Ice Cider Mojito

The Mojito, a beloved Cuban cocktail, is a timeless blend of refreshing mint, zesty lime, and crisp rum. Our take on this classic is inspired by the innovation of mixologist Lynnette Marrero, known for her creative twists on traditional recipes.

Lynnette's influence extends the Mojito's tropical allure, embracing flavors that transport you to sun-soaked beaches and lush landscapes. This rendition pays homage to the Mojito's cultural roots while introducing a contemporary and exotic flair.

Recipe:

Ingredients:
- 2 oz white rum
- 1 oz ice cider
- 1 oz pineapple juice
- 1 oz fresh lime juice
- 1/2 oz simple syrup
- Fresh mint leaves
- Soda water
- Ice cubes

Instructions:
1. In a glass, muddle fresh mint leaves with simple syrup.
2. Add ice cubes to the glass.
3. Pour in white rum, ice cider, pineapple juice, and fresh lime juice.
4. Stir gently to combine the ingredients.
5. Top with soda water for effervescence.
6. Garnish with a mint sprig.

Serving Notes:
Sip on the Tropical Ice Cider Mojito to experience the fusion of traditional Cuban flavors with a modern tropical twist. It's a delightful journey that captures the essence of leisure and celebration, much like the vibrant spirit of Havana where the Mojito originated.

BONUS RECIPES: SAVORY

Contemporary Ice Cider Recipes inspired by Chinese Cuisine

B1. Hot and Sour Ice Cider Soup

The incorporation of ice cider into this recipe elevates the culinary experience by imparting a nuanced sweetness and subtle complexity to the savory ensemble. As the natural sweetness of ice cider mingles with the rich umami of soy sauce and the tanginess of rice vinegar, a harmonious balance of flavors emerges. This addition not only introduces a delightful sweetness but also contributes a unique fruitiness that complements the earthy shiitake mushrooms and bamboo shoots. The interplay of sweetness, acidity, and savory elements creates a symphony of tastes, while the ice cider, alongside sesame oil, black pepper, and chili flakes, adds depth and richness to the broth. This inventive use of ice cider showcases culinary creativity, transforming a classic soup into a memorable and nuanced dish. Each spoonful of this flavorful creation, garnished with green onions and fresh cilantro, invites a culinary journey that tantalizes the taste buds and leaves a lasting impression.

Ingredients:
- 4 cups chicken or vegetable broth
- 1 cup sliced shiitake mushrooms
- 1/2 cup bamboo shoots, julienned
- 1/2 cup firm tofu, cubed
- 1/4 cup rice vinegar
- 2 tablespoons soy sauce
- 1 tablespoon ice cider
- 1 tablespoon cornstarch, dissolved in 2 tablespoons water
- 1 teaspoon sesame oil
- 1 teaspoon freshly ground black pepper
- 1/2 teaspoon chili flakes (adjust to taste)
- 2 green onions, thinly sliced
- Fresh cilantro leaves for garnish

Instructions:

1. In a pot, bring the chicken or vegetable broth to a simmer over medium heat.

2. Add the sliced shiitake mushrooms, bamboo shoots, and tofu to the simmering broth. Cook for 5 minutes, allowing the flavors to meld.

3. In a small bowl, mix together the rice vinegar, soy sauce, and ice cider. Pour the mixture into the pot, stirring gently.

4. Gradually add the dissolved cornstarch, stirring continuously to avoid lumps. This will help thicken the soup.

5. Season the soup with sesame oil, black pepper, and chili flakes. Adjust the spice level according to your preference.

6. Let the soup simmer for an additional 5-7 minutes, ensuring all ingredients are tender.

7. Taste and adjust the seasoning if necessary. If you desire more sourness, add extra rice vinegar.

8. Just before serving, sprinkle sliced green onions over the soup and garnish with fresh cilantro leaves.

9. Serve hot and enjoy the delightful interplay of warmth and coolness in this Hot and Sour Ice Cider Soup.

Contemporary Ice Cider Recipes inspired by Chinese Cuisine

B2.   Ice Cider Pumpkin Congee

Congee, deeply ingrained in Chinese culinary heritage, traces its roots back thousands of years. Originating as a simple rice porridge, congee has evolved into a versatile dish, cherished for its comforting nature and adaptability. Originally consumed as a nourishing staple, congee has transformed over centuries, offering a canvas for creativity in the kitchen.

Our Ice Cider Pumpkin Congee introduces a contemporary twist to this age-old classic. Building on the comforting base of slow-cooked rice, we infuse the dish with the rich and concentrated sweetness of ice cider—an unconventional touch that elevates the flavor profile. The addition of locally sourced pumpkin adds a harmonious blend of earthy undertones, contributing both texture and a vibrant burst of color to this culinary masterpiece.

Ingredients:
- 1 cup Arborio rice or short-grain rice
- 4 cups chicken or vegetable broth
- 1 cup pumpkin puree
- 1/4 cup ice cider
- 1 teaspoon fresh ginger, grated
- 1/2 teaspoon ground cinnamon
- 1/4 teaspoon ground nutmeg
- Salt and pepper to taste
- 2 green onions, thinly sliced (for garnish)
- Toasted pumpkin seeds (for garnish)

Instructions:
1. In a large pot, combine rice and broth. Bring to a boil, then reduce heat to low, cover, and simmer for about 30 minutes, stirring occasionally.

2. Stir in the pumpkin puree, ice cider, grated ginger, ground cinnamon, and ground nutmeg. Continue to simmer for an additional 15-20 minutes, or until the rice reaches a creamy consistency.

3. Season with salt and pepper to taste, adjusting the spices as needed.

4. Before serving, ladle the congee into bowls and garnish with sliced green onions and toasted pumpkin seeds for added texture and flavor.

5. Serve the Ice Cider Pumpkin Congee hot, savoring the harmonious blend of creamy rice, earthy pumpkin, and the subtle sweetness from the ice cider.

Notes:
The first simmer for the Ice Cider Pumpkin Congee is specified as approximately 30 minutes. This duration is suitable for cooking the Arborio rice or short-grain rice until it achieves a partially cooked state. During this initial simmer, the rice absorbs some of the broth and begins to release starch, contributing to the creamy texture of the congee.

It's important to note that the rice will undergo further cooking and absorption during the subsequent steps of adding pumpkin puree, ice cider, grated ginger, ground cinnamon, and ground nutmeg. The additional 15-20 minutes of simmering mentioned in the instructions allows these flavors to meld, the rice to continue cooking, and the congee to reach its desired creamy consistency.

An important note is that this recipe is designed to build layers of flavor and texture over the course of the entire cooking process. The first simmer of 30 minutes sets the stage, and the subsequent steps enhance the dish's richness and complexity.

Contemporary Ice Cider Recipes inspired by Japanese Cuisine
B3.   Seafood & Miso Ice Cider Soup

In this enticing seafood miso soup, the fusion of flavors is a culinary symphony that dances across the palate. The rich depth of a seafood broth, whether fish or shrimp-based, forms the savory foundation, while a touch of ice cider introduces a subtle sweetness, creating a delicate balance. Miso paste, soy sauce, and rice vinegar contribute layers of umami, saltiness, and acidity, weaving together a complex tapestry of taste. Sesame oil adds a nutty richness, complementing the freshness of ginger and garlic. Assorted seafood, shiitake mushrooms, bok choy, and firm tofu absorb the broth's complexity, offering a medley of textures. Garnished with sliced green onions and fresh cilantro, this harmonious ensemble creates a delightful dish, perfect over cooked rice or noodles, inviting diners to savor each spoonful of this flavorful and comforting creation.

Ingredients:
- 4 cups seafood broth (fish or shrimp-based)
- 1/4 cup ice cider
- 2 tablespoons miso paste (white or red)
- 1 tablespoon soy sauce
- 1 tablespoon rice vinegar
- 1 tablespoon sesame oil
- 1 tablespoon fresh ginger, finely grated
- 2 cloves garlic, minced
- 1 cup assorted seafood (shrimp, scallops, mussels, etc.)
- 1 cup shiitake mushrooms, sliced
- 1 cup bok choy, chopped
- 1 package (about 200g) firm tofu, cubed
- 2 green onions, thinly sliced (for garnish)
- Fresh cilantro leaves (for garnish)
- Cooked rice or noodles (optional, for serving)

Instructions:
1. In a pot, combine seafood broth, ice cider, miso paste, soy sauce, rice vinegar, sesame oil, ginger, and garlic. Bring to a gentle simmer over medium heat, stirring to dissolve the miso paste.

2. Add the assorted seafood, shiitake mushrooms, bok choy, and tofu to the simmering broth. Cook for 5-7 minutes or until the seafood is cooked through.

3. Taste the broth and adjust the seasoning if needed, adding more miso, soy sauce, or rice vinegar according to your preference.

4. Ladle the Miso Ice Cider Seafood Soup into bowls. If desired, serve over cooked rice or noodles.

5. Garnish with sliced green onions and fresh cilantro leaves for a burst of color and freshness.

6. Enjoy this flavorful and comforting soup, where the umami of miso, the sweetness of ice cider, and the richness of seafood come together in a symphony of tastes.

This innovative soup recipe showcases the evolution of ice cider from its wintry origins to a versatile ingredient in contemporary culinary creations, providing a delightful and unique dining experience.

Contemporary Ice Cider Recipes inspired by Indonesian Cuisine

B4. Nasi Goreng Ice Cider Fried Rice

Experience the allure of a classic Indonesian *Nasi Goreng*, a dish deeply embedded in culinary history. This rendition pays homage to tradition, marrying fragrant spices and textures that define Indonesian cuisine. What sets it apart is the addition of ice cider, introducing a uniquely sweet complexity that elevates the dish to a new level of appeal and innovation.

Nasi Goreng, translating to "fried rice" in Indonesian, unfolds as a culinary journey steeped in tradition. Originating as a clever solution to repurpose leftover rice, this dish has evolved into an Indonesian culinary icon. Its roots extend from bustling street vendors to home kitchens, embodying the inventive spirit of Indonesian cooking with a harmonious blend of aromatic spices, diverse textures, and layered flavors.

Ingredients:
- 3 cups cooked jasmine rice (preferably day-old)
- 2 tablespoons vegetable oil
- 1 onion, finely chopped
- 3 cloves garlic, minced
- 1 cup cooked and shredded chicken or prawns
- 1 cup mixed vegetables (carrots, peas, corn)
- 2 eggs, beaten
- 3 tablespoons soy sauce
- 1 teaspoon *sambal oelek* (chili paste), optional
- Salt and pepper to taste
- 1/4 cup ice cider
- Green onions, sliced, for garnish
- Fried shallots, for garnish
- Lime wedges, for serving

Instructions:
1. Heat vegetable oil in a wok or large skillet over medium-high heat.

2. Add chopped onions and minced garlic, sautéing until fragrant and golden.

3. Stir in the shredded chicken or prawns and mixed vegetables, cooking until the vegetables are tender.

4. Push the ingredients to one side of the wok, pour the beaten eggs into the empty space, and scramble until just set.

5. Add the day-old jasmine rice to the wok, breaking up any clumps and ensuring it's well-mixed with the other ingredients.

6. In a small bowl, mix together soy sauce and *sambal oelek* (if using). Pour the mixture over the rice and stir well to coat evenly.

7. Pour in the ice cider, infusing a uniquely sweet complexity into the dish. Stir to incorporate.

8. Season with salt and pepper to taste. Continue cooking, stirring frequently, until the rice is heated through and has absorbed the flavors.

9. Garnish the *Nasi Goreng* with sliced green onions and fried shallots.

10. Serve hot with lime wedges on the side, celebrating the rich history and innovative twist of this Indonesian culinary masterpiece.

Contemporary Ice Cider Recipes inspired by Indonesian Cuisine

B5.a. Rendang Puffs with Ice Cider Glaze

Savor the rich and aromatic allure of *Rendang* Puffs, a culinary gem from Indonesian cuisine, elevated with a modern touch. These delectable puffs are uniquely crowned with an enticing Ice Cider Glaze, offering a tantalizing blend of traditional spices and contemporary sweetness.

Rendang, originating from the Minangkabau people of Indonesia, is a slow-cooked meat dish renowned for its complexity of flavors. Traditionally prepared during festive occasions, this culinary masterpiece involves simmering meat in coconut milk and a medley of spices until it achieves a caramelized perfection. *Rendang* symbolizes the rich cultural heritage of Indonesia, reflecting the meticulous care and time devoted to crafting each savory bite.

Ingredients:
- 2 cups shredded beef (cooked *Rendang*)
- Puff pastry sheets (store-bought or homemade)
- 1 egg, beaten (for egg wash)
- Sesame seeds (for garnish)

For the Ice Cider Glaze:
- 1/4 cup ice cider
- 2 tablespoons soy sauce
- 1 tablespoon honey
- 1 teaspoon grated fresh ginger
- 1 teaspoon rice vinegar
- 1/2 teaspoon sesame oil

Instructions:
1. Preheat the oven according to the puff pastry package instructions.

2. Roll out the puff pastry sheets and cut them into squares.

3. Place a spoonful of shredded beef (cooked *Rendang*) onto each puff pastry square.

4. Fold the pastry to form a triangle, sealing the edges. Use a fork to press down and secure the edges.

5. Brush the tops of the pastry with beaten egg and sprinkle with sesame seeds.

6. Bake the *Rendang* puffs in the preheated oven according to the puff pastry package instructions or until golden brown.

7. While the puffs are baking, prepare the Ice Cider Glaze. In a small saucepan, combine ice cider, soy sauce, honey, grated fresh ginger, rice vinegar, and sesame oil. Simmer over low heat until the glaze thickens slightly.

8. Once the puffs are baked and golden, remove them from the oven and let them cool for a few minutes.

9. Drizzle the Ice Cider Glaze over the warm *Rendang* puffs.

10. Serve the *Rendang* Puffs with Ice Cider Glaze as a delightful appetizer or party snack, celebrating the fusion of timeless Indonesian flavors with a contemporary twist.

Contemporary Ice Cider Recipes inspired by Indonesian Cuisine
B5.b.   Making the Rendang Beef, Itself

Traditionally prepared during festive occasions, this slow-cooked beef dish symbolizes the meticulous care and time dedicated to crafting each savory bite. The blend of galangal, ginger, lemongrass, and an array of spices showcases the deep connection between Indonesian culture and the vibrant flavors that define its culinary heritage.

Ingredients:
- 2 lbs beef, thinly sliced or cubed
- 2 cans (27 oz) coconut milk
- 4 stalks lemongrass, bruised
- 4 kaffir lime leaves
- 3 turmeric leaves (optional)
- Salt, to taste
- Coconut oil, for cooking

For the Spice Paste:
- 5 shallots
- 5 cloves garlic
- 3 red chilies (adjust for spice preference)
- 2 inches galangal, peeled
- 1 inch ginger, peeled
- 1 tsp ground turmeric
- 1 tsp ground coriander
- 1/2 tsp ground cumin
- 1/2 tsp cinnamon
- 3 cloves
- 3 cardamom pods

Instructions:
1. In a food processor, blend all the spice paste ingredients until a smooth paste forms.

2. Heat coconut oil in a large, heavy-bottomed pot. Add the spice paste and sauté over medium heat until fragrant.

3. Add the sliced or cubed beef to the pot, stirring to coat the meat in the spice paste.

4. Pour in the coconut milk and add lemongrass, kaffir lime leaves, turmeric leaves (if using), and salt to taste. Stir well.

5. Bring the mixture to a boil, then reduce the heat to low. Simmer uncovered, stirring occasionally, until the coconut milk thickens and the beef becomes tender and caramelized. This process may take 2-3 hours.

6. As the liquid reduces, continue to stir to prevent sticking. Adjust salt if needed.

7. Once the beef is fork-tender and the coconut milk has thickened, remove from heat.

8. Serve the *Rendang* Beef over steamed rice or with traditional Indonesian accompaniments. Or, ideally, with the Rendang Puffs with Ice Cider Glaze!

9. Enjoy the symphony of flavors in this slow-cooked masterpiece that encapsulates the essence of Indonesian culinary heritage.

Contemporary Ice Cider Recipes inspired by Indonesian Cuisine
B6. Gado-Gado with Ice Cider Peanut Dressing

Indulge in the vibrant medley of *Gado-Gado*, a traditional Indonesian salad elevated with a contemporary twist. This refreshing dish features a crisp assortment of vegetables, tofu, and boiled eggs, harmonized by an enticing Ice Cider Peanut Dressing that adds a delightful sweetness and complexity to every bite.

Gado-Gado, translating to "mix-mix" in Indonesian, traces its roots to the diverse culinary landscape of the archipelago. This salad is a celebration of Indonesia's rich agricultural bounty, showcasing an array of fresh vegetables, tofu, and eggs. Traditionally accompanied by a peanut dressing, *Gado-Gado* embodies the country's penchant for balancing flavors and textures in a single, satisfying dish. The addition of ice cider to the peanut dressing brings a contemporary touch to this classic recipe, enhancing its complexity with a subtle sweetness.

Ingredients:
- Assorted fresh vegetables (cabbage, bean sprouts, spinach, cucumber, etc.)
- Firm tofu, cubed and pan-fried
- Hard-boiled eggs, halved
- Rice cakes, sliced (optional)
- *Krupuk* (shrimp crackers), for garnish (optional)

For the Ice Cider Peanut Dressing:
- 1 cup roasted peanuts, finely ground
- 1/4 cup ice cider
- 2 tablespoons soy sauce
- 1 tablespoon tamarind paste
- 1 tablespoon palm sugar or brown sugar
- 1 clove garlic, minced
- 1 red chili, finely chopped (optional)
- Salt, to taste

Instructions:
1. Prepare the vegetables by blanching or steaming until crisp-tender. Arrange them on a serving plate.

2. Pan-fry the cubed tofu until golden brown on all sides.

3. Arrange the tofu and hard-boiled eggs on the plate with the vegetables. Add sliced rice cakes and *krupuk* if desired.

4. In a blender or food processor, combine roasted peanuts, ice cider, soy sauce, tamarind paste, palm sugar, garlic, red chili (if using), and salt. Blend until smooth.

5. Taste the dressing and adjust the sweetness or saltiness as needed.

6. Drizzle the Ice Cider Peanut Dressing generously over the *Gado-Gado* just before serving.

7. Garnish with additional chopped peanuts and a wedge of lime if desired.

8. Serve immediately, allowing the refreshing flavors of *Gado-Gado* with Ice Cider Peanut Dressing to transport you to the heart of Indonesian culinary tradition with a modern twist.

Contemporary Ice Cider Recipes inspired by Hawaiian Cuisine

B7. Ice Cider Glazed SPAM Musubi with Macadamia Nut Crust

Experience a sophisticated twist on Hawaiian comfort food with Ice Cider Glazed SPAM *Musubi* featuring a surprising Macadamia Nut Crust. This elevated dish captures the essence of fine Hawaiian fusion cuisine, blending the sweet complexity of ice cider with the rich crunch of macadamia nuts for a delightful culinary symphony.

Hawaiian Fusion Cuisine reflects the diverse cultural influences that have shaped the island's culinary landscape. From traditional Polynesian flavors to the introduction of Asian and Western ingredients, Hawaii's fusion cuisine has evolved into a unique tapestry of taste. This dish pays homage to this culinary heritage by re-imagining the beloved SPAM *Musubi* with a sophisticated twist that showcases the island's love for unexpected pairings and elevated ingredients.

Ingredients:
- 1 can SPAM, sliced into rectangular pieces
- 1 cup sushi rice, cooked and seasoned
- 1/4 cup soy sauce
- 1/4 cup ice cider
- 2 tablespoons honey
- 1 cup macadamia nuts, finely crushed
- Nori sheets, cut into strips
- Sesame seeds, for garnish
- Fresh cilantro, chopped, for garnish

For Ice Cider Glaze:
- 1/4 cup ice cider
- 2 tablespoons soy sauce
- 1 tablespoon rice vinegar
- 1 tablespoon honey
- 1 teaspoon grated fresh ginger

Instructions:

1. Preheat the oven to 375°F (190°C).

2. In a skillet over medium heat, pan-fry the SPAM slices until golden brown on both sides. Set aside.

3. In a small saucepan, combine soy sauce, ice cider, honey, and grated ginger for the Ice Cider Glaze. Simmer over low heat until it thickens slightly.

4. Dip each SPAM slice into the Ice Cider Glaze, ensuring it's well-coated. Place the glazed SPAM slices on a plate.

5. In a separate bowl, mix crushed macadamia nuts. Press each glazed SPAM slice into the nuts, coating both sides with the nut crust.

6. On a piece of plastic wrap, lay out a strip of nori. Place a mound of seasoned sushi rice on top.

7. Position a macadamia nut-crusted SPAM slice on the rice, then wrap the nori around the rice and SPAM to form a *musubi*.

8. Repeat the process to make additional *musubi*.

9. Place the *musubi* on a baking sheet, sprinkle sesame seeds on top, and bake in the preheated oven for about 10 minutes, allowing the nuts to toast.

10. Garnish with chopped cilantro and serve warm. Enjoy this unique and elevated SPAM dish that captures the essence of Hawaiian Fusion Cuisine with a surprising combination of ice cider and a macadamia nut crust.

Contemporary Ice Cider Recipes inspired by Latin American Cuisine

B8. Ice Cider Citrus Ceviche

Elevate the classic ceviche experience with a refreshing twist – Ice Cider Citrus Ceviche. This vibrant dish combines the zesty freshness of citrus with the subtle sweetness of ice cider, creating a symphony of flavors that dance on the palate.

Ceviche, a culinary gem with roots tracing back to coastal Latin American cuisine, embodies the art of "cooking" fish in the acidity of citrus juices. This ancient method of preparation has evolved into a worldwide sensation, celebrated for its bright and lively flavors. The addition of ice cider, a product of cold-climate apple orchards, introduces a unique sweetness that harmonizes with the citrus, creating a delightful fusion of tradition and innovation.

Ingredients:
- 1 lb fresh white fish (such as halibut or sea bass), cubed
- 1 cup shrimp, peeled and deveined, chopped
- 1 cup fresh lime juice
- 1/2 cup ice cider
- 1 orange, segmented and chopped
- 1 grapefruit, segmented and chopped
- 1 cucumber, diced
- 1/2 red onion, finely chopped
- 1 jalapeño, seeds removed and finely chopped
- 1/4 cup fresh cilantro, chopped
- Salt and pepper, to taste
- Tortilla chips, for serving

Instructions:

1. In a large bowl, combine the cubed fish and chopped shrimp.

2. Pour the fresh lime juice and ice cider over the seafood. Ensure all pieces are submerged in the citrus mixture. Marinate in the refrigerator for at least 30 minutes or until the seafood turns opaque and "cooked" in the acid.

3. Add the chopped orange, grapefruit, cucumber, red onion, jalapeño, and cilantro to the marinated seafood. Gently toss to combine.

4. Season the ceviche with salt and pepper to taste. Adjust the seasoning as needed.

5. Allow the ceviche to marinate in the refrigerator for an additional 15-30 minutes to allow the flavors to meld.

6. Just before serving, give the ceviche a final stir and taste for seasoning.

7. Serve the Ice Cider Citrus Ceviche in individual bowls or glasses, accompanied by tortilla chips for a delightful contrast in texture.

8. Enjoy the bright and invigorating flavors of this unique ceviche that blends the citrusy tradition with the sweet innovation of ice cider.

Contemporary Ice Cider Recipes inspired by Caribbean Cuisine

B7. Tropical Jerk Chicken Skewers with Ice Cider Mango Glaze

Transport your taste buds to the Caribbean with these elevated Tropical Jerk Chicken Skewers, where traditional flavors meet innovation. The succulent chicken, marinated in a vibrant jerk seasoning, is taken to new heights with a luscious Ice Cider Mango Glaze, creating a fusion dish that captures the spirit of the islands.

Caribbean cuisine is a melting pot of flavors influenced by African, Indigenous, European, and Indian culinary traditions. Jerk seasoning, a hallmark of Caribbean cooking, boasts a fiery blend of spices that marries heat with aromatic herbs. The addition of ice cider to the mango glaze pays homage to the Caribbean's love for bold, tropical ingredients, infusing the dish with a subtle sweetness and complexity that elevates the dining experience.

Ingredients:
For the Jerk Chicken:
- 2 lbs boneless, skinless chicken thighs, cut into chunks
- 3 tablespoons jerk seasoning (store-bought or homemade)
- 2 tablespoons olive oil
- 2 tablespoons soy sauce
- 2 tablespoons lime juice
- 2 cloves garlic, minced
- Wooden skewers, soaked in water

For the Ice Cider Mango Glaze:
- 1 cup ice cider
- 1 ripe mango, peeled and diced
- 2 tablespoons honey
- 1 tablespoon Dijon mustard
- 1 teaspoon grated fresh ginger
- 1 lime, zest and juice
- Salt and pepper, to taste

Instructions:

1. In a bowl, mix together jerk seasoning, olive oil, soy sauce, lime juice, and minced garlic to create the marinade.

2. Toss the chicken chunks in the jerk marinade, ensuring they are well-coated. Cover and refrigerate for at least 2 hours, allowing the flavors to infuse.

3. While the chicken is marinating, prepare the Ice Cider Mango Glaze. In a saucepan, combine ice cider, diced mango, honey, Dijon mustard, grated ginger, lime zest, and lime juice. Simmer over medium heat until the mango is softened and the mixture has thickened. Season with salt and pepper to taste.

4. Preheat the grill or grill pan.

5. Thread the marinated chicken chunks onto soaked wooden skewers.

6. Grill the jerk chicken skewers until cooked through and slightly charred on the edges.

7. During the last few minutes of grilling, baste the chicken skewers with the Ice Cider Mango Glaze, ensuring they are well-coated.

8. Serve the Tropical Jerk Chicken Skewers with additional Ice Cider Mango Glaze on the side for dipping.

9. Enjoy this Caribbean-inspired elevated dish that harmonizes the bold flavors of jerk seasoning with the sweet sophistication of ice cider and mango.

Contemporary Ice Cider Recipes inspired by Argentinian Cuisine
B8. Chimichurri Ice Cider Marinade for Grilled Steak

Take your grilled steak to new heights with a Chimichurri Ice Cider Marinade, a zesty and herbaceous blend that infuses the richness of grilled meat with the sweet complexity of ice cider. This Argentine-inspired marinade elevates the grilling experience to a symphony of bold flavors.

Chimichurri, a staple in Argentine cuisine, traces its roots to the gauchos and their love for open-fire cooking. This vibrant sauce combines fresh herbs, garlic, and tangy vinegar to create a robust condiment that complements grilled meats. The addition of ice cider to the marinade brings a modern twist, infusing a layer of sweetness that balances the sharpness of the chimichurri, creating a harmonious and memorable dining experience.

Ingredients:
For the Chimichurri Ice Cider Marinade:
- 1 cup fresh parsley, finely chopped
- 1/2 cup fresh cilantro, finely chopped
- 4 cloves garlic, minced
- 1/2 cup extra-virgin olive oil
- 1/4 cup red wine vinegar
- 1/4 cup ice cider
- 1 teaspoon dried oregano
- 1 teaspoon red pepper flakes (adjust to taste)
- Salt and black pepper, to taste

For the Grilled Steak:
- 2 lbs sirloin or ribeye steak
- Salt and black pepper, to season

Instructions:

1. In a bowl, combine chopped parsley, chopped cilantro, minced garlic, red wine vinegar, ice cider, dried oregano, red pepper flakes, salt, and black pepper.

2. Slowly whisk in the extra-virgin olive oil until the mixture emulsifies. Adjust salt and pepper to taste.

3. Reserve a portion of the chimichurri marinade for serving and refrigerate it.

4. Place the steak in a shallow dish and generously coat it with the Chimichurri Ice Cider Marinade. Ensure the meat is well-covered. Marinate in the refrigerator for at least 2 hours, or preferably overnight, to allow the flavors to permeate.

5. Preheat the grill to medium-high heat.

6. Remove excess marinade from the steak and season with additional salt and black pepper.

7. Grill the steak to the desired doneness, turning once to achieve grill marks.

8. Let the steak rest for a few minutes before slicing.

9. Serve the grilled steak drizzled with the reserved Chimichurri Ice Cider Marinade.

10. Enjoy the delectable fusion of Argentine tradition and modern innovation in this Chimichurri Ice Cider Marinade, bringing an elevated twist to your grilled steak experience.

Contemporary Ice Cider Recipes inspired by Creole Cuisine
B9. Creole Ice Cider Jambalaya

Ignite your taste buds with a modern twist on the classic Creole dish – Creole Ice Cider Jambalaya. This elevated recipe combines the robust flavors of the bayou with the sweet depth of ice cider, creating a harmonious and memorable dining experience.

Creole cuisine, rooted in the vibrant culture of New Orleans, is a flavorful tapestry woven with influences from French, Spanish, African, and Caribbean culinary traditions. Jambalaya, a beloved Creole dish, reflects this rich amalgamation of flavors. The addition of ice cider to this recipe brings a contemporary touch, infusing a layer of sweetness that complements the smoky and spicy undertones of Creole spices, offering a unique and elevated twist to this iconic dish.

Ingredients:
For the Creole Ice Cider Sauce:
- 1/2 cup ice cider
- 1 can (14 oz) diced tomatoes
- 1 onion, finely chopped
- 1 bell pepper, diced
- 3 celery stalks, chopped
- 3 cloves garlic, minced
- 2 tablespoons tomato paste
- 1 teaspoon Creole seasoning
- 1 teaspoon smoked paprika
- 1/2 teaspoon dried thyme
- 1/2 teaspoon cayenne pepper (adjust to taste)
- 1 bay leaf
- Salt and black pepper, to taste
- 2 tablespoons vegetable oil

For the Jambalaya:
- 1 lb chicken thighs, boneless and skinless, cut into chunks
- 1 lb andouille sausage, sliced
- 1 lb shrimp, peeled and deveined
- 2 cups long-grain white rice
- 4 cups chicken broth
- 1 cup okra, sliced (fresh or frozen)
- 2 green onions, sliced
- Fresh parsley, chopped, for garnish

Instructions:

1. In a large, heavy pot, heat vegetable oil over medium heat. Add chopped onions, diced bell peppers, and chopped celery. Sauté until vegetables are softened.

2. Stir in minced garlic, tomato paste, Creole seasoning, smoked paprika, dried thyme, cayenne pepper, and bay leaf. Cook for 2-3 minutes until the spices are fragrant.

3. Pour in ice cider and diced tomatoes (with their juice). Season with salt and black pepper. Simmer for 10-15 minutes until the sauce thickens.

4. In the same pot, add chicken chunks and andouille sausage. Cook until the chicken is browned.

5. Stir in rice and cook for 2-3 minutes, allowing the rice to absorb the flavors.

6. Pour in chicken broth and bring the mixture to a boil. Reduce heat to low, cover, and simmer for 15-20 minutes or until the rice is almost cooked.

7. Add shrimp and sliced okra to the pot. Cover and simmer for an additional 5-7 minutes until the shrimp are pink and opaque.

8. Adjust seasoning as needed. Remove the bay leaf.

9. Garnish with sliced green onions and chopped parsley.

10. Serve this Creole Ice Cider Jambalaya hot, allowing the unique blend of Creole spices and sweet ice cider to transport you to the heart of New Orleans.

Contemporary Ice Cider Recipes inspired by Pacific Northwest Cuisine

B10. Pacific Northwest Ice Cider-Infused Dungeness Crab Risotto with Chanterelle Mushrooms and Edible Gold Leaf

Elevate your dining experience with a decadent dish inspired by the Pacific Northwest – Ice Cider-Infused Dungeness Crab Risotto. This luxurious creation combines the delicate sweetness of Dungeness crab with the complexity of ice cider, enriched further by earthy chanterelle mushrooms and a touch of opulence with edible gold leaf.

The Pacific Northwest's culinary heritage is deeply entwined with the bounty of the sea and the lush forests that characterize the region. Dungeness crab, a celebrated local delicacy, serves as the focal point of this dish. Ice cider, a product of the region's apple orchards, introduces a unique sweetness that complements the richness of the crab and the savory notes of the risotto. This luxurious rendition pays homage to the Pacific Northwest's commitment to exceptional ingredients and culinary innovation.

Ingredients:
For the Ice Cider-Infused Dungeness Crab Risotto:
- 1 cup Arborio rice
- 1/2 cup dry white wine
- 4 cups seafood or vegetable broth, kept warm
- 1 shallot, finely chopped
- 2 tablespoons unsalted butter
- 1 tablespoon olive oil
- 1/2 cup ice cider
- 1 cup Dungeness crabmeat, picked
- 1/2 cup chanterelle mushrooms, cleaned and sliced
- 1/4 cup grated Parmesan cheese
- Salt and white pepper, to taste

For Garnish:
- Edible gold leaf
- Fresh chives, chopped
- Lemon wedges

Instructions:

1. In a large skillet, heat olive oil and 1 tablespoon of butter over medium heat. Add the chopped shallot and sauté until translucent.

2. Add Arborio rice to the skillet and stir to coat the rice with the oil and butter. Cook for 2-3 minutes until the rice becomes slightly translucent at the edges.

3. Pour in the dry white wine and cook until it is mostly absorbed by the rice.

4. Begin adding the warm seafood or vegetable broth, one ladle at a time, stirring frequently. Allow the liquid to be absorbed before adding the next ladle. Continue this process until the rice is creamy and cooked to al dente.

5. In the final stages of cooking, add the ice cider to the risotto, stirring continuously.

6. In a separate pan, sauté the chanterelle mushrooms in the remaining butter until they are golden brown and cooked through.

7. Fold the Dungeness crabmeat and sautéed chanterelle mushrooms into the risotto.

8. Stir in grated Parmesan cheese and season the risotto with salt and white pepper to taste.

9. To serve, plate the Ice Cider-Infused Dungeness Crab Risotto, garnish with edible gold leaf, and sprinkle with fresh chives.

10. Serve immediately with lemon wedges on the side for a luxurious and elevated Pacific Northwest dining experience.

BONUS RECIPES: DESSERTS

Contemporary Ice Cider Dessert Recipes

D1   Ice Cider and Mixed Fruit Frozen Custard

Frozen custard, originating in the early 20th century, embodies a smoother and creamier evolution in frozen desserts. Incorporating ice cider, a beverage rooted in cold-climate apple-growing regions, adds a contemporary twist. Ice cider itself, with a history linked to regions with freezing temperatures, enhances this recipe, marrying modern culinary innovation with timeless flavors. Whether enjoyed as a homemade delight or a social gathering centerpiece, this dessert harmonizes regional ingredients and culinary traditions, celebrating the evolving landscape of sweet creations.

Ingredients:

- 1 cup whole milk
- 1 cup heavy cream
- 3/4 cup granulated sugar
- 4 large egg yolks
- 1/2 cup ice cider
- 1 teaspoon vanilla extract
- 1 cup mixed fresh fruits (such as diced apples, pears, and berries)

Instructions:

1. Prepare the Ice Cream Base:
   - In a medium saucepan, heat the whole milk and heavy cream over medium heat until it just begins to simmer. Do not let it boil.
   - In a separate bowl, whisk together the sugar and egg yolks until well combined.

2. Temper the Eggs:
   - Gradually pour a small amount of the hot milk mixture into the egg mixture, whisking constantly. This process, called tempering, prevents the eggs from curdling.
   - Slowly pour the tempered egg mixture back into the saucepan with the remaining hot milk, stirring continuously.

3. Cook the Custard:
   - Cook the custard over medium-low heat, stirring constantly, until it thickens enough to coat the back of a spoon. Be careful not to let it boil.
   - Once thickened, remove the custard from heat and strain it through a fine-mesh sieve into a clean bowl.

4. Add Ice Cider and Vanilla:
   - Stir in the ice cider and vanilla extract into the custard. Let the mixture cool to room temperature, then cover it and refrigerate for at least 4 hours or overnight.

5. Freeze the Custard:
   - Churn the custard in an ice cream maker according to the manufacturer's instructions.
   - During the last few minutes of churning, add the mixed fresh fruits to the ice cream maker.

6. Transfer and Freeze:
   - Transfer the churned custard with fruit into a lidded container. Cover the surface with parchment paper or plastic wrap before sealing the container with a lid.
   - Freeze the custard for at least 4 hours or until firm.

7. Serve and Enjoy:
   - Scoop the Ice Cider and Fruit Frozen Custard into bowls or cones.
   - Garnish with additional fresh fruit or a drizzle of extra ice cider if desired.

Contemporary Ice Cider Dessert Recipes

D2   Ice Cider Sabayon

The roots of *sabayon*, a French and Italian dessert, date back centuries, showcasing a tradition of indulgence. Ice cider, born from regions with frigid winters that naturally concentrate apple sugars, adds a contemporary twist. This fusion represents a convergence of historical culinary techniques and regional specialties, delivering a dessert that resonates with both tradition and innovation.

Ingredients:
- 4 large egg yolks
- 1/2 cup granulated sugar
- 1/2 cup ice cider
- Fresh berries for garnish

Instructions:

1. In a heatproof bowl, whisk together egg yolks and sugar until pale and fluffy.

2. Place the bowl over a pot of simmering water (double boiler) and gradually whisk in the ice cider.

3. Continue whisking constantly until the sabayon thickens and forms ribbons when lifted.

4. Remove from heat and let it cool slightly.

5. Serve the Ice Cider Sabayon in individual glasses, garnished with a selection of fresh berries.

6. Enjoy this delightful dessert, a perfect blend of historical elegance and modern flavor.

Contemporary Ice Cider Dessert Recipes
D3   Ice Cider Poached Fig and Mascarpone Parfait

The parfait, a French dessert with layered perfection, finds its roots in the late 19th century. It symbolizes a delicate balance of flavors and textures. Ice cider, a contemporary addition, brings a unique sweetness, while the art of poaching figs harkens back to ancient culinary traditions. This dessert is a testament to the evolution of classic techniques meeting modern palates.

Ingredients:
- 6 ripe figs, halved
- 1 cup ice cider
- 1/4 cup honey
- 1 cup mascarpone cheese
- 1/4 cup powdered sugar
- 1 teaspoon vanilla extract
- Crushed pistachios for garnish

Instructions:

1. In a saucepan, combine the figs, ice cider, and honey. Simmer over medium heat until figs are tender (about 10 minutes).

2. Remove figs and reduce the poaching liquid to a syrupy consistency. Let both cool.

3. In a bowl, whisk together mascarpone, powdered sugar, and vanilla until smooth.

4. In serving glasses, layer mascarpone mixture, poached figs, and a drizzle of the ice cider reduction.

5. Repeat the layers, finishing with a sprinkle of crushed pistachios on top.

6. Chill parfait for at least 2 hours before serving.

7. Delight in the harmonious blend of poached figs, mascarpone, and ice cider—a journey through time in every bite.

Contemporary Ice Cider Dessert Recipes
D4   Ice Cider Apple Crisp

The humble apple crisp, a comfort food staple, has roots tracing back to early American cuisine. Its evolution mirrors the simplicity and resourcefulness of generations past. Ice cider, a modern touch, introduces a layer of complexity to this classic dessert. This fusion pays homage to the enduring appeal of apple-based sweets and the innovation that continues to shape our culinary landscape.

Ingredients:
- 6 cups peeled and sliced apples (a mix of sweet and tart varieties)
- 1/2 cup ice cider
- 1 tablespoon lemon juice
- 1/2 cup granulated sugar
- 1 teaspoon ground cinnamon
- 1/2 cup all-purpose flour
- 1/2 cup rolled oats
- 1/2 cup brown sugar
- 1/4 cup cold unsalted butter, diced
- Vanilla ice cream for serving

Instructions:

1. Preheat the oven to 350°F (175°C).

2. In a large bowl, toss the sliced apples with ice cider, lemon juice, granulated sugar, and ground cinnamon.

3. Transfer the apple mixture to a baking dish, spreading it evenly.

4. In a separate bowl, combine flour, rolled oats, brown sugar, and diced butter. Mix until crumbly.

5. Sprinkle the crumb mixture evenly over the apples.

6. Bake for 40-45 minutes or until the top is golden brown, and the apples are tender.

7. Allow it to cool for a few minutes before serving.

8. Serve the Ice Cider Apple Crisp warm, topped with a scoop of vanilla ice cream for a delightful contrast.

9. Enjoy this comforting dessert that bridges the past and present with the timeless flavor of apples and the contemporary twist of ice cider.

Contemporary Ice Cider Dessert Recipes

D5 Ice Cider and Balsamic Roasted Strawberries with Ricotta

The roots of this innovative dessert trace back to the rich tapestry of culinary history, where the convergence of diverse ingredients and culinary techniques has yielded timeless creations. The cultivation of strawberries, a fruit beloved for its delicate sweetness, can be traced to ancient Rome, where it was considered a symbol of love and prosperity.

As the centuries unfolded, the art of preserving fruits evolved. The discovery of ice cider, a beverage born from regions with frigid climates that naturally concentrate apple sugars, stands as a testament to the ingenuity of cold-climate apple-growing regions. This unique elixir, which became popular in recent decades, carries echoes of traditional apple-based libations that have roots in regions such as Quebec, Canada, and the northeastern United States.

Balsamic vinegar, a staple in Mediterranean cuisine, has its origins in Italy, where it has been crafted for centuries. Initially produced in small batches for personal use, it later gained popularity and became a sought-after condiment that added depth and complexity to various dishes.

The combination of these historical elements in the Ice Cider and Balsamic Roasted Strawberries with Ricotta reflects a contemporary twist on age-old traditions. Roasting strawberries with the marriage of ice cider and balsamic vinegar pays homage to the time-honored practice of preserving fruits, while the addition of creamy ricotta introduces a layer of sophistication inspired by Italian and Mediterranean culinary heritage.

This dessert not only showcases the evolution of culinary techniques but also the global exchange of flavors and ideas. It invites us to savor the interplay between history and innovation, creating a sensory experience that transcends time and place. In each bite, we taste the culmination of centuries of culinary exploration and cultural amalgamation, a sweet symphony of flavors that resonates across the ages.

Ingredients:

2 cups fresh strawberries, halved
1/4 cup ice cider
2 tablespoons balsamic vinegar
2 tablespoons honey
1 cup ricotta cheese

Instructions:

1. Preheat the oven to 375°F (190°C).

2. Toss strawberries with ice cider, balsamic vinegar, and honey.

3. Roast for 15-20 minutes until strawberries are caramelized.

4. Serve the roasted strawberries over a dollop of ricotta.

Contemporary Ice Cider Dessert Recipes
D6   Ice Cider and Rosewater Granita

The story of this enchanting dessert unfolds against the backdrop of centuries-old culinary practices and the evolution of refreshing frozen treats. The tradition of crafting frozen desserts can be traced back to ancient China, where inventive minds used ice and snow to create icy delights. Over time, this practice spread to various corners of the world, each region infusing its unique flavors and techniques into frozen concoctions.

The introduction of ice cider into this recipe brings us to the cold-climate apple-growing regions of North America, particularly in places like Quebec, Canada, and the northeastern United States. Here, the serendipitous combination of freezing temperatures and apple orchards gave rise to the production of ice cider. This contemporary elixir is a nod to the historical methods of concentrating fruit flavors in cold climates, echoing the resourcefulness of our ancestors.

Rosewater, a fragrant distillation of rose petals, finds its origins in ancient Persia. Over the centuries, it traveled along the Silk Road, influencing culinary traditions in the Middle East, North Africa, and Southern Europe. The delicate floral essence of rosewater became a symbol of refinement, used in both sweet and savory dishes to elevate the sensory experience.

The Ice Cider and Rosewater Granita, therefore, is a marriage of these diverse historical elements. It merges the ancient art of freezing with the modern innovation of ice cider, creating a dessert that encapsulates the essence of cold climates and apple orchards. The addition of rosewater, with its storied journey through cultural exchanges, adds a layer of aromatic sophistication.

In each spoonful of this granita, one can taste the echoes of ancient China, the resilience of cold-climate apple growers, and the fragrant whispers of Persian gardens. It is a testament to the enduring appeal of frozen delights and the timeless dance of flavors that transcends borders and eras. Enjoy this frozen symphony, a harmonious blend of history, innovation, and the sheer pleasure of a cool, refreshing treat.

Ingredients:

- 2 cups ice cider
- 1/4 cup sugar
- 1 tablespoon rosewater

Instructions:

1. Mix ice cider, sugar, and rosewater until sugar dissolves.

2. Pour the mixture into a shallow dish and freeze.

3. Every 30 minutes, scrape the mixture with a fork until it forms a fluffy, icy texture.

4. Serve in glasses and garnish with edible flowers.

Contemporary Ice Cider Dessert Recipes

D7 Canadian-inspired Ice Cider Butter Tart Cheesecake

The creation of this uniquely Canadian dessert pays homage to the nation's rich culinary heritage, where diverse influences have shaped a tapestry of flavors over the centuries. Canada, with its expansive landscapes and varied climates, has been a melting pot of indigenous traditions and immigrant contributions, resulting in a vibrant and distinctive culinary identity.

The roots of this dessert extend back to the Indigenous peoples of Canada, who had a deep connection with the land and its bounty. Traditional ingredients such as maple syrup and berries played a significant role in their cuisine, offering both sustenance and symbolism. As European settlers arrived, they brought with them culinary traditions that further enriched the Canadian gastronomic landscape.

The concept of butter tarts, a quintessentially Canadian treat, emerged in the late 19th to early 20th century. The exact origin is debated, but it is widely agreed that this gooey, sweet confection became a cherished part of Canadian dessert culture. The combination of buttery goodness, sweet filling, and often pecans or raisins showcases the amalgamation of European and North American influences.

Ice cider, a more recent addition to the Canadian culinary scene, reflects the country's commitment to innovation in agriculture and beverage production. The cold-climate apple-growing regions of Canada, particularly in Quebec and the Maritimes, have become renowned for producing high-quality ice cider. This sweet elixir, created through a process of naturally concentrating apple sugars during freezing temperatures, adds a contemporary touch to traditional flavors.

The fusion of these elements in the Canadian-inspired Ice Cider Butter Tart Cheesecake is a celebration of the nation's culinary journey. The graham cracker crust pays homage to European cheesecake traditions, while the incorporation of ice cider and the nod to butter tarts represent a modern twist on beloved classics. The pecan and maple syrup toppings echo the longstanding connection to Canada's natural resources.

Ingredients:

- 1 1/2 cups graham cracker crumbs
- 1/2 cup melted butter
- 2 packages cream cheese, softened
- 1 cup sugar
- 1/4 cup ice cider
- 1 teaspoon vanilla extract
- Pecan halves and maple syrup for topping

Instructions:

1. Mix graham cracker crumbs with melted butter and press into the base of a cheesecake pan and preheat your oven to 325°F (163°C).

2. In a bowl, beat cream cheese, sugar, ice cider, and vanilla until smooth.

3. Pour the cream cheese mixture over the crust.

4. Bake until set, then let it cool and refrigerate.

5. Before serving, top with pecan halves and drizzle with maple syrup.

Contemporary Ice Cider Dessert Recipes

D8 Indian-inspired Ice Cider Gulab Jamun Trifle

This inventive dessert draws inspiration from the opulent tapestry of Indian culinary history, a legacy that spans millennia and reflects the diverse cultural influences that have shaped the subcontinent. Indian sweets, or *"mithai,"* have been an integral part of the country's gastronomic heritage, evolving over time to become an art form in their own right.

Gulab Jamun, the star of this trifle, is a classic Indian sweet believed to have originated in medieval Persia. As trade routes expanded, this delectable treat found its way to the Indian subcontinent, where it underwent various regional adaptations. Comprising deep-fried dough balls soaked in a sugar syrup infused with cardamom and rose water, *Gulab Jamun* encapsulates the essence of sweet indulgence in Indian celebrations.

The infusion of ice cider into this traditional treat introduces a contemporary twist, reflecting the global exchange of culinary ideas in modern times. Ice cider, with its roots in cold-climate apple-growing regions such as Quebec and the northeastern United States, brings a unique sweetness that harmonizes with the rich flavors of *Gulab Jamun*.

Trifles, with their layers of cake, cream, and fruit, have their own European heritage. The melding of Indian and European influences in this dessert symbolizes the dynamic interplay between culinary traditions across continents.

In the Indian-inspired Ice Cider *Gulab Jamun* Trifle, each layer tells a story—a story of centuries-old sweets, of trade routes that connected diverse cultures, and of contemporary innovations that bridge traditional and modern flavors. The trifle becomes a canvas where the colors and aromas of India meet the crisp sweetness of ice cider, creating a sensory experience that transcends time and borders.

As you indulge in this dessert, you embark on a journey through the annals of Indian culinary history, celebrating the artistry of *mithai* and the evolving global palate that continues to shape the world of sweets. It's a symphony of flavors, a harmonious dance between the past and the present, inviting you to savor the sweet melodies of a cross-cultural culinary masterpiece.

Ingredients:

- *Gulab jamun* (store-bought or homemade)
- 1 cup ice cider
- 1 cup thickened saffron-infused condensed milk
- Chopped pistachios for garnish

Instructions:

1. Soak *gulab jamun* in ice cider until they absorb the flavor.

2 In serving glasses, layer soaked *gulab jamun* with saffron-infused condensed milk.

3. Repeat the layers and garnish with chopped pistachios.

4. Refrigerate for a few hours before serving.

Contemporary Ice Cider Dessert Recipes
D8b   Making Gulab Jamun

Indian sweet dessert traditions trace their roots to ancient times, deeply intertwined with cultural, religious, and social practices. The advent of sugarcane cultivation in the Indian subcontinent around 300 BCE marked the beginning of sweet-making endeavors.

Halwa, an ancient sweet, has references in Sanskrit literature, and jaggery-based sweets were enjoyed even during the Vedic period. However, it was during the medieval period that Persian and Central Asian influences introduced intricately crafted sweets, including the beloved *Gulab Jamun*.

Gulab Jamun's name is derived from Persian words, with *"gulab"* meaning rose and *"jamun"* referring to a fruit with a similar size and shape. Over time, this delicacy became an integral part of Indian celebrations, symbolizing sweetness and joy.

The Mughal influence further enriched Indian sweets with innovations like the introduction of *"shahi tukda"* and *"jalebi."* Sweets such as *Rasgulla* and *Sandesh* from the eastern regions, *Laddu* from the south, and *Barfi* from the north showcase the diverse regional flavors and preparations.

The art of making Indian sweets is often passed down through generations, with each family having its closely guarded recipes. These sweets play a central role in festivals, weddings, and other joyous occasions, symbolizing prosperity, happiness, and the richness of Indian culinary heritage.

Ingredients:

For *Gulab Jamun*:
- 1 cup milk powder
- 1/4 cup all-purpose flour
- 1/4 cup *ghee* (clarified butter)
- 2 tablespoons milk
- 1/4 teaspoon baking soda
- A pinch of cardamom powder
- *Ghee* or oil for frying

For Sugar Syrup (replace with ice cider if making the Indian-inspired Ice Cider *Gulab Jamun* **Trifle recipe, D8):**
- 1 cup sugar
- 1/2 cup water
- A few strands of saffron (optional)
- 1/2 teaspoon rose water

Instructions:

1. In a mixing bowl, combine milk powder, all-purpose flour, *ghee*, baking soda, and cardamom powder.

2. Add milk gradually, kneading the mixture into a soft dough. If needed, add more milk to achieve a smooth consistency.

3. Divide the dough into small portions and roll them into round balls, ensuring they are smooth and crack-free.

4. Heat *ghee* or oil in a pan over medium heat. Fry the dough balls until golden brown, maintaining a medium-low temperature to ensure even cooking.

5. In a separate saucepan, combine sugar and water for the syrup. Bring it to a boil, stirring until the sugar dissolves.

6. Add saffron strands and simmer for a few minutes until the syrup thickens slightly.

7. Remove the syrup from heat, add rose water, and let it cool slightly.

8. Soak the fried dough balls in the warm sugar syrup for at least an hour, allowing them to absorb the sweetness.

Contemporary Ice Cider Dessert Recipes
D9   African-inspired Ice Cider Rooibos Panna Cotta

The creation of an African-inspired dessert like Ice Cider Rooibos Panna Cotta is a testament to the rich and diverse culinary traditions that span the vast and varied landscapes of the African continent. Culinary heritage in Africa is deeply intertwined with the land, its people, and the unique flavors that have evolved over centuries.

Rooibos, a key component of this dessert, is native to the Cederberg region of South Africa. Indigenous Khoisan peoples first discovered this herbal plant and began brewing a tea from its leaves. Over time, rooibos gained popularity not only for its unique flavor but also for its perceived health benefits. The infusion of rooibos in culinary creations pays homage to a plant deeply rooted in African soil.

Panna Cotta, a classic Italian dessert, reflects the influence of European culinary traditions. The intersection of European and African flavors in this dessert mirrors the complex history of cultural exchanges that occurred through trade, colonization, and migration.

Ice cider, while not native to Africa, brings a contemporary touch to this recipe. Its inclusion speaks to the modern era of global culinary exploration, where ingredients from different corners of the world can harmonize to create new and exciting flavor profiles. This addition represents the ongoing dialogue between traditional and innovative culinary practices.

Assembling these elements into an Ice Cider Rooibos Panna Cotta bridges the historical and the contemporary, creating a dessert that tells a story of cultural interplay. The creamy texture of panna cotta, the earthy notes of rooibos, and the sweet complexity of ice cider come together in a celebration of flavors that transcends borders.

In each spoonful of Ice Cider Rooibos Panna Cotta, one can savor the echoes of ancient brewing techniques, the melding of European and African culinary legacies, and the exploration of new possibilities in the modern kitchen. This dessert is a reminder that the culinary journey is dynamic, fluid, and always evolving, reflecting the diversity and resilience of the people who have shaped its narrative over the ages. It invites us to appreciate not only the flavors on our plates but also the cultural stories they carry, fostering a deeper understanding of the interconnected world of food and history.

Ingredients:

- 2 cups rooibos tea, cooled
- 1/2 cup ice cider
- 1/2 cup honey
- 2 teaspoons gelatin
- 1 cup heavy cream
- Fresh berries for topping

Instructions:

1. Bloom gelatin in ice cider and let it dissolve.

2. Combine cooled rooibos tea, honey, and gelatin mixture.

3. In a separate bowl, whip heavy cream until stiff peaks form.

4. Fold whipped cream into the tea mixture.

5. Pour into molds or glasses and refrigerate until set.

6. Top with fresh berries before serving.

Contemporary Ice Cider Dessert Recipes
D10   Ice Cider Gilded Nectar Cocktail

This extravagant cocktail harmonizes the rich warmth of aged rum with the intricate sweetness of ice cider reduction and the citrusy brightness of Grand Marnier and fresh lemon juice. The addition of edible gold leaf elevates the presentation, turning each sip into a luxurious experience. The Gilded Nectar Cocktail is a celebration of ice cider's versatility, depth, and its ability to transform an ordinary cocktail into an extraordinary sensory masterpiece. Enjoy this opulent creation as a sophisticated finale to an elegant evening.

Ingredients:

For the Ice Cider Reduction:
- 2 cups high-quality ice cider
- 1/4 cup honey
- 1 cinnamon stick
- 1 star anise

For the Cocktail:
- 1 1/2 oz premium aged rum
- 1 oz ice cider reduction
- 1/2 oz Grand Marnier
- 1/2 oz freshly squeezed lemon juice
- Ice cubes
- Edible gold leaf for garnish
- Orange peel twist for garnish

Instructions:

1. Prepare the Ice Cider Reduction:
   - In a saucepan, combine ice cider, honey, cinnamon stick, and star anise.
   - Simmer over low heat until the mixture reduces to a thick, syrupy consistency.
   - Allow it to cool and strain to remove spices.

2. Crafting the Cocktail:
   - In a mixing glass, combine the premium aged rum, ice cider reduction, Grand Marnier, and freshly squeezed lemon juice.
   - Add ice cubes and stir gently to chill the mixture.

3. Strain and Serve:
   - Strain the cocktail into a chilled coupe or martini glass.

4. Garnish with Elegance:
   - Gently place a delicate sheet of edible gold leaf on the surface of the cocktail, allowing it to float gracefully.
   - Express the oils from an orange peel twist over the drink by giving it a quick twist, then drop it into the glass.

5. Sip and Savor:
   - The Gilded Nectar Cocktail is best enjoyed slowly, allowing the layers of flavors to unfold on the palate.

Final Thoughts

In crafting this inaugural cookbook, "The Ice Cider Epic," we embarked on a culinary odyssey to match the innovation and spirit inherent in the creation of ice cider itself. It has been a thrilling endeavor, exploring the rich tapestry of historical eras and diverse cuisines, both traditional and contemporary, all woven together with the golden elixir of ice cider.

As we delve into these pages, we hope to inspire a community of ice cider devotees, food enthusiasts, and chefs eager to embrace this extraordinary ingredient as one of the world's great culinary treasures. May these recipes spark creativity, elevate your culinary experiences, and offer a taste of the unparalleled depth and versatility that ice cider brings to the kitchen.

To those who dare to experiment, to chefs who seek new frontiers, and to all who appreciate the magic of culinary alchemy, we extend our heartfelt wishes. May your kitchens be filled with the sweet notes of ice cider, and may the journey through these pages ignite a passion for crafting, creating, and savoring the culinary wonders that ice cider can unlock.

Cheers to the boundless possibilities that lie ahead, as we raise a glass to the future of ice cider in the world of gastronomy. May your culinary adventures be as rich and vibrant as the golden nectar that has inspired this epic journey.

Happy crafting and happy cooking!

www.ingramcontent.com/pod-product-compliance
Lightning Source LLC
Chambersburg PA
CBHW050732010526
44107CB00010B/820